Balance for Busy Single Moms

Creating Positive Patterns to

Thrive with Joy

Heather Eden

Dedication

To the radiant constellation of single mothers who have illuminated my path during the most challenging chapters of my journey. Navigating parenthood alone is a voyage of unparalleled strength and unwavering determination. With heartfelt reverence, this book is affectionately dedicated to:

My extraordinary grandmother, a fearless maverick with an unbreakable soul, who fearlessly raised nine children single-handedly.

My beloved Aunt Rose, who traversed the intricate terrain of single parenthood, eventually finding love anew and gracing us with two more precious lives.

To every woman co-navigating parenthood while carrying the weight of solitude, and to the widows who radiate unshakable grace and resilience in the face of profound loss.

To the mothers within marriages who courageously confront isolation and the apprehension of shouldering parenthood alone.

To the exceptional mothers surmounting the added challenge of disabilities, your bravery and affection shine brighter than any obstacle.

Unified by diverse experiences, strengths, and hues, single mothers, this book stands as an homage to your relentless spirit.

For the mothers who've sensed inadequacy, remember you are a masterpiece in progress, and your expedition is marked by bravery, optimism, and unyielding love. This book is a living testament to our shared fortitude and a persistent reminder to hold onto faith. Continue forging ahead, for our collective journey knows no bounds. Persevere, always.

With deep admiration and unbreakable solidarity,

Heather Eden

CONTENTS

About the Author

Heather Eden stands as a radiant exemplar of resilience and unwavering determination, epitomizing the very essence of her roles as a Licensed Professional Counselor and a Certified Health Coach. As the dedicated single mother of two exceptionally bright and remarkable individuals, Heather's life voyage stands as a profound testament to her indomitable fortitude and unyielding commitment.

Her insightful prose and empowering counsel have positioned Heather as a wellspring of inspiration for mothers navigating the intricate landscape of contemporary existence. The pages of her books, including *"Balance for Busy Moms - A Stress-Free Guide to Tranquility"* and *"Balance for Busy Moms - Cook Your Way to Health,"* reflect her profound comprehension of the myriad challenges mothers encounter. These works present pragmatic, holistic remedies, encapsulating her profound insights into nurturing equilibrium amidst the tumult.

Heather's fervor for aiding others in their quest for

personal excellence radiates through every facet of her being. Leveraging her background as a Licensed Professional Counselor, she has wholeheartedly dedicated herself to furnishing guidance and bolstering individuals striving to surmount hurdles and attain emotional well-being. Her compassionate methodology and seasoned acumen have touched the lives of numerous souls, establishing her as a trusted confidante and a tireless champion of constructive transformation.

Beyond her counseling acuity, Heather's status as a Certified Health Coach signifies her commitment to championing holistic well-being. With profound insight into the intricate interplay between mental and physical wellness, she emboldens individuals to embark on journeys of transformative self-discovery and optimal health attainment.

Heather's resolute commitment to her family's welfare, her unflagging pursuit of personal growth as a single mother, and her achievements as a published author and counselor seamlessly weave into a narrative of triumph over adversity. Fueled by her devotion to her children, her zealous dedication to aiding others, and her unrelenting quest for harmony, she emerges as a luminous source of inspiration for mothers universally.

Heather Eden's odyssey reminds us that even within the crucible of life's trials, we possess the potential to effect profound change. Her narrative and contributions continue to stir hearts and elevate spirits, leaving an enduring imprint on those who have had the privilege of crossing her path.

Page Blank Intentionally

Preface

"Balance for Busy Single Moms: Creating Positive Patterns to Thrive with Joy," was born from a place of heartfelt purpose and a deep personal connection. As both a Licensed Professional Counselor (LPC) and a single mother raising two exceptional children, I hold a close understanding of the intricate challenges that single mothers face each day. This book embodies my own experiences, professional wisdom, and an unshakable commitment to making a positive impact in the lives of single mothers who, like me, find themselves gracefully juggling numerous responsibilities while striving to nurture their own well-being.

Through my role as an LPC, I've had the humbling privilege of working closely with individuals, diving into their struggles, and bearing witness to their transformative journeys toward healing and growth. Yet, it was my own path as a single mother that truly ignited a deep-seated desire to create a resource that could empower, uplift, and guide other single moms toward a path of serenity, fulfillment, and abundance.

Within the pages of "Balance for Busy Single Moms," I weave together a tapestry of personal insights and professional know-how to directly address the specific challenges that single mothers encounter. From managing the constraints of time and financial demands to nurturing one's own mental and emotional well-being, I am intimately acquainted with the overwhelming nature of these pressures. Yet, I firmly believe that within these challenges lie the seeds of opportunity to cultivate positive patterns that lead to both inner peace and external abundance.

I hold a profound recognition that the journey of a single mother is both deeply personal and shared among many. This book extends beyond simple advice; it is a heartfelt sharing of empathy for the struggles, paired with practical tools and strategies that I am confident can truly make a difference. I've personally witnessed the transformative power of positive habits, mindfulness techniques, and self-care practices in my own life and in the lives of those I've had the privilege to counsel.

"Balance for Busy Single Moms" stands as a guiding light, supporting single mothers as they navigate their journey with strengthened resilience, renewed confidence, and a sense of purpose that's been rekindled. My intention is to walk alongside my fellow single mothers as a compassionate ally, offering guidance and serving as a reminder that they are not walking this path alone. I want to inspire them to craft new patterns that cultivate peace, nurture abundance, and ultimately lead to a life that's not only balanced but also deeply enriching.

Through this book, I extend more than advice; I extend a hand of heartfelt support and a voice that warmly assures, "You can triumph, thrive, and discover joy in your unique journey as a single mother."

Chapter 1: Creating a Spiritual Life

Prayer, meditation, spiritual laws, and moral laws are integral elements of a fulfilling spiritual life. These concepts provide a foundation for the right action, thought, and being, serving as a guide for making ethical and meaningful choices in our daily lives. By incorporating these practices into our daily routine, we can connect with a higher being and tap into inner wisdom to gain clarity, peace, and motivation and achieve our set goals. The spiritual laws and moral laws help us understand our place in the world and how our actions can positively impact us and those around us. With this understanding, we can live a life grounded in purpose, integrity, and compassion. Let us get going with learning about each of these things and their effects on our lives.

Word of the Lord says, *"I am the vine; you are the branches. If you remain in me and I in you, you will bear much fruit; apart from me, you can do nothing."* First thing first, to ensure that everything we do bears fruit, it is important that we remain in the Lord and consequently create and maintain a spiritual life so that we can continue to be on the right road to achieving our goals. God is our fountain of strength and direction; hence we must abide in Him and practice the way of the Lord if we want to have a consistent lifestyle and reap the healthy fruits of our efforts in various aspects of our lives. Obeying God's commands and following His ways can dramatically bless every aspect of our lives, as stated in the Book of Deuteronomy, chapter 28.

I understand that nourishing the Spirit is not always an easy endeavor since we live in a world that progressively trends toward secularism, materialism, and commercialism. Today's difficulty is figuring out how to nurture, nourish, heal, repair, and regenerate the soul in a world that is not conducive to spiritual development. I agree that doing so is not easy, but it is not impossible. The good news is that the Word of God gives us absolute directions on how we can build or restore our relationship with God, along with real-life examples for our encouragement and motivation. God knows that we may face challenges and temptations can be at the door, and therefore, He is always there for all those who genuinely want to root their lives spiritually.

In this chapter, we will talk about some strategies and steps you can take to strengthen yourselves spiritually and keep steadfast.

First of all you must develop an everyday prayer routine Prayer is an essential spiritual practice for many people, and having a daily prayer routine can help establish a regular habit of connecting with one's spiritual beliefs. According to 75% of Americans, prayer is a significant component of their everyday lives. Because they have witnessed and personally experienced the advantages that regular prayer brings to your life. Daily prayer can help us to establish a sense of connection to something greater than ourselves, whether that be a higher power, the natural world, or one's inner self. It also enhances our sense of purpose. Taking time to reflect on our beliefs and values can help clarify our sense of purpose and direction in life. In times of difficulty and despair, prayer or talking to God gives us comfort and a sense of support.

Making prayer our lifestyle does not only have spiritual benefits, but it has a significantly positive impact on our physiological health. According to medical professionals who have studied the physiological benefits of prayer, respiration is controlled, and blood pressure and heart rate are balanced during prayer, which consequently helps us feel more in control and at peace while reducing stress.

When our spiritual, mental, emotional, and physiological health is all at its optimum, we begin to sense inner peace and tranquility. Hence not only for the sake of our souls but also for improving mental and emotional well-being, a daily prayer routine can help to reduce stress, anxiety, and depression and can improve one's overall emotional well-being.

By being thankful to God for everything in your prayers, He will bless you more abundantly; and when discussing your life matters with God becomes part of your daily routine, your life will begin to take a positive turn. It's a divine result of positive, committed action aligned with the universal law of motion. Moreover, what we intentionally do with our time matters. The deeper your connection becomes from intentional practice and seeing positive results, the more you will begin to rely on God more than your efforts and understanding, and God will start working in your life beyond your imagination. "The miracles are a broad spectrum, and they may vary from subtle ones to magnificent ones, like God calming a storm in your life or turning 100.00 dollars into a fortune".

The Bible tells us that God listens to the prayers of a righteous person (1 Peter 3:12, Proverbs 15:29, James 5:16). Therefore, when you pray, expect God to work around your request, and it will eventually come out as a miracle. The significance of requesting miracles can vary depending on

4

an individual's beliefs and spiritual practices. However, for many people, requesting miracles can be a powerful way to connect with a higher power and express deep faith and trust in the divine. We experience miracles every day in the form of:

- **Small acts of kindness,** such as a kind word or gesture from a stranger, a friend, or a loved one, can be a subtle miracle that brings joy and positivity to our day.

- **Synchronicities:** When we pray to God and ask for His will for any given matter in our life, such as while making a decision or amid the fulfillment of a goal, He miraculously works things out, indicating if/if not, it is His will. It can be seen as subtle miracles that guide us on our path.

- **Healing:** Physical or emotional recovery, even if it is small or gradual, is considered a miracle. You may be suffering an unfortunate incident in your life and gradually realize that you have come a long way through strengthening your relationship with the Lord and with unceasing supplications. The tears you once shed are finally rewarded.

- **Answered prayers:** Answered prayers are considered miracles as they are the fulfillment of our requests and wishes placed before God's altar, often in unexpected ways, showing that God is listening and providing guidance and support. They remind us that we are not alone and our prayers are heard. Sometimes they may not be fulfilled immediately, in which is the purpose of faith and patience.

- **A sense of protection and safety:** Feeling protected and safe, even in uncertain or dangerous circumstances, is a miracle because anxiety is a common response to such a situation. When you can feel safe, it means that God, who is beyond all circumstances, is at work for you.

Experiencing a miracle can build us spiritually in several ways. It can deepen our faith, increase hope and positivity, empower us, remind us to be grateful, show love and concern for others, and connect us with God, who is more significant than ourselves, ultimately leading to spiritual growth. As we advance in our spiritual journey, we become more attuned to the workings of a higher power. These subtle miracles that may have gone unnoticed before become more pronounced in our consciousness, and we can clearly see how they are guiding us toward our greater good.

Moreover, it is crucial to consider the intent behind the request. Some may see it as a way to control the outcome of a situation and avoid personal responsibility. Additionally, it is essential to remember that miracles may not always come in the form we expect. Therefore, we must be open to the possibility of unexpected blessings and trust that whatever form the miracle takes is for our highest good.

God is in all people and manifests His divine power through communicating love to all persons. "For You have wrought all our works in us, Lord" (Isaiah 26:12). Therefore, connecting with a community through a church, a fellowship, or a casual gathering where you discuss and learn about things and purposes in common can positively impact one's sense of meaning and purpose. Being a part of a community can provide a sense of belonging and support, which can be especially important during times of stress or hardship and combat loneliness. Additionally, participating in religious or spiritual practices with a community can provide a sense of connection to something greater than oneself and can foster feelings of peace and contentment. Furthermore, being part of a community can also provide opportunities for service and giving back, which can be a powerful source of fulfillment and personal growth. Overall, connecting with a community can provide a sense of belonging, support, and purpose that can be beneficial for individuals on their spiritual journey. Most importantly, creating community in your life aids comfort and safety during times of crisis.

All these elements will help us to be closer to God. Remember establishing a relationship with God is a two-way channel of communication where we participate through prayer- talking to God- and we listen in stillness. That is why we must spend quiet time with God so that He can speak to us. We must be able to clear our minds from the voices of the world so we can hear His voice when He speaks. The Word of God says, *be still and know that I am God*- Psalms 46:10. Once you have created a personal connection with the Lord, you will learn how to recognize His voice.

With time you will figure out that talking and listening to God on a daily basis is pretty amazing. It's a way to build connections and receive guidance and support for our lives. Checking in with God throughout the day is also a great way to stay in tune with your higher self. It can be as formal as ritual prayers or chatting with God in your mind. It's a way of telling God how grateful we are, what we're hoping for, and what's freaking us out. And in return, we can get comfort, wisdom, and inspiration. The more we do it, the more we build trust in God and in ourselves. Plus, building a connection with the Creator of the Universe builds confidence and nourishes love and hope. Let's not forget; prayer gives us a chance to reflect on what's important and figure out what we want to do and what we need to let go of. Hearing what God has to communicate to us is as crucial as pouring out our hearts to Him.

This is where meditation fits! In the stillness of our thoughts, He communicates to us for our growth and to impart peace. It helps us cultivate quietness in our lives by teaching us to slow down, be present in the moment, and focus our attention inward. By taking time to meditate regularly, we can develop a greater awareness of our thoughts, emotions, and physical sensations. This heightened self-awareness can help us identify patterns of stress and anxiety and develop skills to manage these distractions. Additionally, meditation helps to reduce the activity of the "monkey mind," which is the constant stream of thoughts and distractions that often prevent us from feeling calm and centered. Through this practice, we can learn to quiet our minds, reduce stress and anxiety, and cultivate a sense of peace and inner stillness. This stillness can have a ripple effect, spilling over into our daily lives and helping us approach even the busiest of days with a greater sense of calm, clarity, and centeredness.

Once we have established a good relationship with the divine being, we continue to realize that everything in the world revolves around the interplay of various laws that help us achieve our goals and the way everything else in our surroundings works. This reminds me of the Seven Laws of the Universe. The Seven Spiritual Laws of the Universe are a set of principles that offer an understanding of the relationship between the individual self and the universe. These laws were first outlined in the book "The Seven Spiritual Laws of Success" by Deepak Chopra and provide a framework for living a fulfilling and successful life. The laws include:

1. **The Law of Pure Potentiality:** This law states that every individual has access to the infinite field of pure potentiality, which is the source of all creation.

2. **The Law of Giving and Receiving:** This law states that in order to receive, one must first give. Giving and receiving are different aspects of the same flow of energy.

3. **The Law of Karma:** This law states that every action has a consequence and that the universe is constantly balancing and rebalancing itself.

4. **The Law of Least Effort:** This law states that the universe operates with effortless ease and that the

individual should strive to live in a state of effortless grace and ease.

5. **The Law of Intention and Desire:** This law states that every individual has the power to manifest their desires through the alignment of their intentions with the universe.

6. **The Law of Detachment:** This law states that detachment is necessary for true abundance and that by letting go of attachment to the outcome, one can manifest their desires more easily.

7. **The Law of Dharma:** This law states that every individual has a unique purpose or path in life and that by aligning with one's dharma, one can achieve fulfillment and success.

Each of these laws impacts us in its unique way depending on how we implement and apply them in our lives. Discussed below are a few examples for each law:

1. **The Law of Pure Potentiality** enables individuals to unlock their innermost aspirations and harmonize them with the cosmic force of creation, thereby actualizing their aspirations.

2. **The Law of Giving and Receiving** instructs individuals to focus on the act of giving rather than receiving, thereby fostering a mindset of abundance.

3. **The Law of Karma** enlightens individuals to the understanding that every action bears a corresponding repercussion and that they are accountable for crafting the reality they experience.

4. **The Law of Least Effort** teaches individuals to live in a state of effortless poise and ease and to relinquish resistance and struggle.

5. **The Law of Intention and Desire** aids individuals in aligning their intentions with the universe, thereby effortlessly manifesting their desires.

6. **The Law of Detachment** instructs individuals to relinquish attachment to the outcome, thereby achieving their goals with minimal stress and struggle.

7. **The Law of Dharma** guides individuals to comprehend their unique purpose or path in life, thereby providing a sense of direction and fulfillment.

Lastly, we all must remember that no matter which belief we identify or which religious values we abide by, we all live in a world of diverse values. Each of us is fighting our own battle, and we must be just and kind to each other. Therefore, instead of tearing each other down, we must utter words of kindness and encourage each other to pursue righteous paths so we all can enjoy the goodness bestowed on us by the Lord. Never letting down each other's morale must be one of our goals, as motivating each other to do good is our motto so we all can develop a good living place in this world.

Kant's moral philosophy offers valuable guidance for individuals looking to improve their decision-making and behavior. By following the "categorical imperative," individuals can learn to act in ways that align with the universal laws of morality. This means that individuals should ask themselves before making any decision or taking action that will affect another. "Would I be willing to see everyone else act this way?" Doing so can ensure that their actions are respectful and considerate towards others.

Furthermore, this principle encourages individuals to treat others with respect and dignity in all aspects of their lives. It helps individuals to understand that their actions have an impact on others and to be mindful of the way they treat others. This can lead to deeper connections with others and more meaningful and fulfilling relationships.

Similarly, Cooperative behavior is a powerful tool

for individuals looking to improve their relationships and achieve personal and collective success. At its core, cooperative behavior is about working together for the common good and recognizing that our actions have an impact on those around us. By embracing this concept, individuals can learn to prioritize collaboration, compromise, and mutual respect in their interactions with others. This can help build stronger and more meaningful personal and professional relationships. Collaboration allows individuals to combine their unique skills and strengths to achieve a common goal. The compromise allows them to find solutions that work for everyone involved, while mutual respect fosters trust and understanding.

Additionally, adopting a cooperative mindset can contribute to creating a more harmonious and prosperous society. By working together, individuals can address complex social issues and create a better future for themselves and those around them.

Perhaps based on the same theories, Oxford University came up with seven universal moral rules:

i. Do not harm others,
ii. Do not lie,
iii. Do not steal,
iv. Do not cheat,

v.   Do not abuse power,

vi. Do not betray the trust and

vii. Do not treat others unjustly.

These rules are intended to guide moral behavior and decision-making and are based on the principles of fairness, empathy, and respect. Nonetheless, all of them have their roots in the Ten Commandments, given to Moses by God.

All of these different approaches to morality share the common goal of promoting ethical behavior and decision-making. While each approach may have its own unique focus or emphasis, they all share the fundamental principles of fairness, empathy, and respect. These principles are essential for creating a just and harmonious society and for fostering personal growth and self-awareness.

All in all, we must realize the importance of developing a daily prayer and meditation routine, as it strengthens our spiritual life and helps us maintain a connection to the divine. We must realize that prayer and meditation have both spiritual and physical benefits, such as reducing stress and anxiety and co-creating various miracles in life. Yes. We have been created in the image of God; so shall we create. However, how incredible the feeling to be aligned with the divine and experience real-time creation(s) with the omnipotent and omnipresent Spirit, the One with an eternal embodiment of love and power. How great is this opportunity? It's truly one of the most remarkable experiences of being human. Don't miss out!

Forbye, The Law of Action, moral laws, and universal spiritual laws all play a role in shaping our thoughts, behaviors, and overall mindset. The Law of Action emphasizes the importance of taking concrete steps toward our goals and desires, reminding us that manifestation requires action, not just thoughts and intentions. Moral laws support acting with integrity and righteousness, while universal spiritual laws help us understand the power of intention and energy. When we combine the understanding and application of these laws with regular prayer and meditation, we are able to connect with the divine and align our minds, body, and soul. This alignment can lead to a greater sense of peace and understanding, as well as the manifestation of our desires.

Moreover, Dr. Joe Dispenza, a chiropractor, researcher, and author in the field of brain science and epigenetics, is best known for his work on the connection between the mind, body, and soul and how this connection can be harnessed through practices like meditation and prayer to promote personal growth and spiritual development.

Dr. Dispenza's research suggests that the mind and body are interconnected and that our thoughts and emotions can profoundly impact our physical health. He argues that by using techniques like meditation and prayer, we can access a state of consciousness that allows us to release limiting beliefs and negative emotions that are holding us back in life. This, in turn, can lead to improved physical, emotional, and spiritual well-being. Meditation and prayer are powerful tools for accessing this state of consciousness because they quiet the mind and allow us to focus on the present moment. This focus helps us to connect with our inner self, tap into the power of the universe, and access a higher state of consciousness.

In summary, Dr. Joe Dispenza's research highlights the importance of the connection between the mind, body, and soul and how it can be harnessed through practices like meditation and prayer to promote personal growth and spiritual development. By accessing this state of consciousness, we can release limiting beliefs and negative emotions and tap into the power of the universe, AKA divine energy or God's presence, to improve our physical, emotional, and spiritual well-being. Therefore, enjoy creating a positive pattern called a routine of prayer and meditation, and witness your life upgrade to higher levels.

Chapter 2: Reduce and Manage Stress

Stress is an inevitable part of life. Whether it's caused by work, relationships, health issues, or just the daily grind, we all experience stress to some degree. And while a certain amount of stress can be motivating and even beneficial, too much of it can take a toll on our mental and physical health. In fact, chronic stress has been linked to a range of health problems, including anxiety, depression, heart disease, and obesity which is why it is so important to learn how to manage and reduce our stress levels.

As a single mom, you are likely to face a unique set of challenges that can cause stress. Whether it is financial worries, juggling multiple responsibilities, or feeling like you're not doing enough. These pressures can take a toll on your mental and physical well-being. But the truth is, stress is a normal part of life, and it's essential to recognize that you're not alone in feeling this way. In fact, studies show that many single moms experience high levels of stress, and it's nothing to be ashamed of unless and until you are able to recognize it and have the insight to do something about it.

By learning to manage your stress levels, you can improve your overall quality of life and become a happier, healthier, and more resilient parent.

In this chapter, I will guide you through the causes and effects of stress and provide you with practical strategies to help you manage and reduce it. From mindfulness practices to healthy lifestyle habits, such as a yoga self-care routine, I'll offer a range of techniques that you can use to promote relaxation, resilience, and well-being in your life whether you're only dealing with the stress of being a single parent or with tens of other responsibilities as well. These strategies will help you navigate the challenges and find greater peace and balance.

First and foremost, it is essential to acknowledge that seeking professional help for stress is not a sign of weakness. In fact, it's a brave and proactive step towards taking care of your mental and emotional health. Unfortunately, there's still a stigma surrounding therapy or counseling, which can prevent some people from seeking the help they need. But let's throw that stigma out of the window right now because I must say, if you are holding this book in your hand and are still reading this, I know that you want to be helped. Trust me, and there are times when you have to be that helping hand and take a stand for yourself. There is absolutely no shame in reaching out to a mental health professional if you're struggling with stress or any other emotional challenge.

Therapy is a valuable resource that may offer you a safe and supportive setting in which you can talk about your feelings and emotions, develop methods to cope, and strive towards a life that is more fulfilling and healthier. A skilled mental health professional's advice and knowledge can help you negotiate the challenges of stress and other emotional disorders with greater comfort and confidence. When you're dealing with stress, it's easy to feel swamped and alone. However, counseling may provide you with a safe environment to be understood and listened to without fear of judgment or condemnation. You can get better insight into your thoughts and behaviors, as well as discover new strategies to cope with stress and anxiety through talk therapy or other therapeutic techniques.

Since stress can significantly impact your cognition, it is known to activate the body's natural "fight or flight" response, which can result in the release of hormones such as cortisol and adrenaline. These hormones can make you feel even more overwhelmed, exacerbate stress and negatively impact your mental health. Furthermore, they affect the brain's functioning and lead to cognitive changes, such as:

i. **Impaired memory:** Stress can impair memory and make recalling knowledge more difficult.

ii. **Reduced attention span:** When you are worried, concentrating can be difficult, and your attention span may suffer.

iii. **Reduced decision-making capacity:** Stress can impair decision-making ability, leading to indecision and increased anxiety.

iv. **Slowed reaction times:** Stress can slow down your reaction times, making it challenging to respond swiftly to events.

v. **Anxiety:** Chronic stress can induce anxiety, which can negatively impair your cognition and general quality of life.

Now someone who is experiencing chronic stress might engage in black-and-white thinking, where they see situations as either all good or all bad, without any shades of gray. They might also engage in catastrophizing, where they imagine the worst-case scenario in every situation, even when it's unlikely to happen. These cognitive distortions can lead to a negative cycle of thoughts and behaviors impacting not only their lives but also those around them. Especially when you are a single mom and have to tend to kids, you may unconsciously begin to project these patterns on your child/ren.

Indeed, no parent would want to do that, right? Therefore, availing of talk therapy can be an effective way to address these cognitive distortions and promote more rational and balanced thinking. Through this, you can learn to identify and challenge negative thoughts and beliefs and reframe them in a more positive and realistic light. For example, if you tend to catastrophize, a therapist might help you examine the evidence for your catastrophic thoughts and help you come up with a more balanced perspective. They might also teach you relaxation and mindfulness techniques (which we have talked about in Chapter 2) to help you manage these issues.

Once you are done with the second step of seeking professional help and dealing with cognitive distortions, you will automatically upgrade to the third step, which is reasoning to reduce stress. You can say it is the byproduct of addressing cognitive distortions. Your therapist will most likely help you get to this step and provide you with a helping hand, but you have to address the elephant in the room. And before you can move forward, here is a quick reality check. It is true that seeking out resources like books or professional help can be beneficial when trying to manage stress. However, it's important to remember that no matter how much help you receive, progress ultimately comes down to your own determination and effort.

You can read every book on stress management or see the best therapists in the world, but if you're not willing to put in the work and make changes in your own life, these efforts may not be practical. It's crucial to approach stress management with a mindset of commitment and determination and be willing to put in the necessary work to make positive changes in your life. With the right attitude and effort, you can, bit by bit, address any issue that comes your way.

Let us go back to rational thinking. This involves regulating emotions and seeking truth and facts before creating beliefs and acting. When we're under stress, it's easy to become reactive and impulsive, which can lead us to make decisions based on our emotions rather than reason and evidence. We might jump to conclusions or believe things without considering all the facts. This can lead to faulty thinking and poor decision-making.

As a single mom, you might feel overwhelmed and stressed trying to balance work, parenting, and household responsibilities. It's easy to become reactive and impulsive in this situation, which can lead you to make decisions based on your emotions rather than reason and evidence. For example, you might feel guilty for not spending enough time with your children and make impulsive decisions to overcompensate, which can lead to burnout and more stress.

So, while it's important to think rationally and seek truth and facts before making decisions, it's also important to acknowledge and harness your emotions in a healthy way. By finding a balance between reason and emotion, you can improve your ability to manage stress and make better decisions for yourself and your family. Consequently, you will be able to think more rationally and manage stress, and you can take a step back and harness your emotions. Acknowledge that it's natural to feel overwhelmed and stressed and that it's okay to ask for help. Seek truth and facts before creating beliefs and taking action. This means seeking out reliable sources of information and critically evaluating the evidence before coming to a conclusion. It also means being aware of your own biases and assumptions and working to overcome them through self-reflection and critical thinking.

For example, if you feel guilty for not spending enough time with your children, you can seek truth and facts by asking yourself:

i. How much time do I actually spend with my children?

ii. How can I optimize the time I have with them so it's quality time?

iii. What are some ways I can take care of myself so I have the energy to be present with my children?

By seeking truth and facts, you can gain a more accurate understanding of your situation and make better decisions based on reason and evidence to alleviate stress and improve your well-being as a single mom. It's also important to consider your values and reasoning when making decisions. What is most important to you? What are your priorities? How do your beliefs and actions align with your values?

By including these aspects, your questions may sound like this:

i. What are my values and beliefs about parenting, and are they aligned with my actions?

ii. What is the reasoning behind my guilt, and is it based on truth and facts or just my emotions?

Your aim in addressing cognitive distortions is to eradicate the harmful impacts of stress, which are impaired memory, reduced attention span, reduced decision-making capacity, slowed reaction times, and such so that you can think rationally. Many people assume that rational thinking means growing cold of emotions and becoming indifferent. However, that is not the case. When you are able to think rationally, you are able to regulate your emotions well. Your calm and sorted mind will help you analyze which of these emotions are reasonable and which should not be paid too much attention to. However, if irrational emotions or thoughts are becoming intrusive or frequent, please consult with your therapist.

Your goal is to acknowledge and manage your emotions in a healthy way for which you are stamping out cognitive distortions and developing a rational mind. Therefore, you must not wholly put aside your emotions and feelings. Instead, it means learning to recognize and accept your emotions while also taking steps to manage them. Discussed below are a few healthy approaches that you can use to harness your emotions and create positive responses to negative criticism throughout your journey as a single parent.

1. **Recognize Your Triggers:** The journey starts with recognizing what triggers strong emotional responses in you. Take some time to pay attention to how you feel and react to different situations or people. This awareness will help you identify your triggers so you can prepare yourself to manage them effectively.

   For example: If you know that public speaking triggers anxiety for you, you can prepare yourself by practicing deep breathing exercises or visualization techniques beforehand. This will help you regulate your emotions and feel more confident when giving a presentation.

   In this way, you can feel more in control of your emotions and better equipped to manage negative feedback. Remember that regulating your emotions takes practice and patience, but it's a skill that can greatly enhance your well-being and relationships with others.

2. **Prioritize Self-Care Activities:** Prioritizing self-care activities like exercise, meditation, or spending time in nature can help regulate your emotions. Research shows that spending time in green spaces can reduce stress and improve mood. Whether it's

going for a walk in a local park, hiking in the mountains, or simply sitting outside in a garden, being in nature can help you feel more relaxed and grounded. Exercise releases tension and boosts mood, while meditation calms the mind and improves emotional regulation. Spending time in nature reduces stress and improves mood. By prioritizing self-care, you can improve your emotional regulation skills and feel more equipped to handle challenging situations.

3. **Calming Exercises:**

Calming exercises like progressive muscle relaxation involve tensing and relaxing different muscle groups in your body to release tension and promote relaxation. This technique helps you become more aware of physical sensations in your body and can be an effective way to reduce stress and promote relaxation. Similarly, Guided imagery and visualization techniques are both powerful tools for regulating your emotions and promoting relaxation. Guided imagery involves creating a mental image of a peaceful environment or scene, while visualization techniques involve mentally rehearsing a positive outcome or experience. Both techniques involve using your imagination to promote positive emotions and reduce stress.

4.   Deep Breathing/ Grounding:

When it comes to regulating your emotions, deep breathing and grounding techniques can be incredibly helpful tools to have in your toolkit. Deep breathing, for example, is a simple and effective way to calm your mind and reduce stress. By taking slow, deep breaths, you can activate your body's relaxation response, which can help you feel calmer and more centered. This, in turn, can help you better manage your emotions, especially when you're feeling overwhelmed or anxious.

Grounding techniques, on the other hand, can help you feel more present and in control of your emotions by increasing your awareness of the present moment. The "5-4-3-2-1" grounding practice employs your senses to help you feel more present and in control of your emotions. You may practice naming five things you can see, four things you can feel, three things you can hear, two things you can smell, and one item you can taste. This exercise can help with anxiety management and can be done anywhere, at any time.

5. **Seek support:** Seeking support from a therapist or counselor can be an important step towards harnessing your emotions in a healthy way. Sometimes, it can be hard to cope with intense emotions on your own, and that's completely okay. After all, we're humans. A trained professional can help you develop healthy coping mechanisms to regulate your emotions since they are skilled at tailoring their approach to your specific needs.

Learning to regulate your emotions takes practice and patience, but it's an essential part of improving your mental and emotional well-being. Celebrating small victories along the way can help keep you motivated to continue practicing these techniques. Remember, taking care of yourself is not selfish; it's necessary to be the best parent you can be for your children. If you don't learn to harness your emotions, you may end up feeling overstimulated and unable to manage the demands of parenting. So, make sure to prioritize your emotional well-being.

When you experience overstimulation, it means you're being bombarded with an excessive amount of sensory input or stress. This can cause your emotions to become heightened, leaving you feeling anxious, stressed, or agitated. In our fast-paced world today, overstimulation is becoming increasingly common, and it can have a significant impact on your mental and emotional well-being.

If you're an anxious parent, you may unknowingly pass on your anxiety to your children. Children learn by example, and they're likely to pick up on your behaviors and emotions. If you're anxious or stressed, your child may learn to feel the same way in similar situations. Over time, this can lead to your child developing their own anxiety disorder. For instance, if you're always worried about your child's safety and constantly checking up on them, your child may learn to become anxious about their own safety. Similarly, if you're anxious about social situations, your child may learn to feel anxious in social situations as well. It's essential for you as a parent to be aware of your own anxiety and to manage it properly so that you do not unintentionally pass it on to your children.

Children who grow up in anxious environments may develop similar anxious traits and behaviors. They may also become more reserved and avoidant of social situations, as they may have learned to associate social situations with anxiety and stress. Moreover, children of anxious parents may also develop a heightened sense of fear and worry, making them more susceptible to anxiety disorders later in life. They may struggle with low self-esteem and confidence and may also have difficulty with decision-making and problem-solving. If a child has experienced overstimulation because you reflect that on them, it is probable that they will be emotionally dysregulated. It is crucial to soothe and provide comfort to the child in such a situation. A supportive environment, a structured routine, clear guidance, and encouragement are all necessary for your and your child's well-being.

Your emotions are like powerful energies that can affect every aspect of your life. However, sometimes you struggle to harness these energies, particularly when it comes to the more difficult emotions. When left unchecked, these emotions can build up like a pressure cooker until they inevitably boil over. But what if you could learn to channel and harness these energies in a healthy way? That's where healing therapies come in. Through practices like yoga, sound therapy, art therapy, and dance therapy, you can learn to express and channel your emotions in a positive way, unlocking a new level of emotional intelligence and your overall well-being. By embracing these therapies, you can gain a greater sense of control over your emotions and experience a more fulfilling and balanced life.

I encourage you to introduce these therapies in your daily life and make them your lifestyle. If you practice yoga therapy, you may experience reduced stress levels and improved physical health. This holistic approach integrates physical postures, breathing techniques, meditation, and relaxation, which can help to balance your mind and body. A [1]A study published in the Journal of the International Society of Preventive & Community Dentistry, under the title *"Association of yoga practice and serum cortisol levels in chronic periodontitis patients with stress-related anxiety and depression,"* indicated that People who engage in regular yoga practice showed lower levels of serum cortisol, the hormone associated with stress.

In addition, you may be interested to know that sound therapy is a powerful tool for promoting relaxation and healing. This approach involves using sound waves to calm your body and reduce stress and anxiety. It is based on the principle that everything in the universe vibrates at a specific frequency, including your body's atoms and molecules. When these vibrations become out of sync, they can cause emotional and physical imbalances. Sound therapy uses instruments like gongs, singing bowls, and tuning forks to

---

[1] Katuri, K. K., Dasari, A. B., Kurapati, S., Vinnakota, N. R., Bollepalli, A. C., & Dhulipalla, R. (2016). Association of yoga practice and serum cortisol levels in chronic periodontitis patients with stress-related anxiety and depression. Journal of International Society of Preventive & Community Dentistry, 6(1), 7–14. https://doi.org/10.4103/2231-0762.175404

create specific frequencies that resonate with different parts of your body, helping to restore balance and harmony. The vibrations can activate your parasympathetic nervous system, which is responsible for your body's rest and relaxation response, further promoting calmness and relaxation. There are also healing frequencies, such as 432 hz to help improve mental clarity and focus. By us tuning into healing frequencies, we can enable physical healing in the body with total relaxation and calmness

Art therapy involves using art materials and techniques to explore emotions, promote self-awareness, and improve mental health. It helps you to express yourself creatively and process difficult emotions in a safe and supportive environment. It also aids to a powerful manifesting tool called the vision board. Vision boards can be created to express your inner most desires of love and personal goals for life. When we see it, we believe it! Likewise, dance therapy is a form of therapy that involves using movement and dance to promote emotional, cognitive, and physical integration. It can help to reduce anxiety and depression, improve self-esteem, and promote a sense of well-being. A review of studies published in Frontiers in

Psychology, titled as [2] *"Effectiveness of Dance Movement Therapy in the Treatment of Adults With Depression: A Systematic Review With Meta-Analyses"* found that dance therapy can be an effective treatment for depression. The authors noted that dance therapy might be particularly effective for individuals who struggle to express their emotions through words.

As you practice healing therapies like yoga, sound, art, and dance therapy, you will experience a range of benefits. These therapies will help alleviate your stress, reduce your anxiety and depression, improve your physical health, and promote emotional balance. It's important that you find a therapist who is trained in the specific therapy you are interested in and who can provide you with guidance and support throughout the healing process, especially in the initial stages.

Once you have turned away from the negatives of your life and have directed your focus to taking care of yourself, you can create a self-care routine which is essential for establishing consistency in the path you have chosen. Most of you will find yourself automatically creating one

---

[2] Karkou, V., Aithal, S., Zubala, A., & Meekums, B. (2019). Effectiveness of dance movement therapy in the treatment of adults with depression: A systematic review with meta-analyses. Frontiers in Psychology, 10, 936. https://doi.org/10.3389/fpsyg.2019.00936

because when you look after yourself, you inevitably end up organizing and advancing your self-care means. These will include incorporating vitamins, supplements, teas, and essential oils into your routine that can help provide your body with the necessary nutrients and support it needs to function at its best. Vitamins and supplements can help boost your immune system, promote healthy skin, and support various body functions. Teas can provide relaxation, reduce stress and anxiety, and even boost your energy levels. Essential oils have therapeutic properties that can promote relaxation, improve mood, and reduce inflammation.

Detoxification is another important aspect of self-care. Detoxing can help eliminate toxins from your body and improve your overall health. You can incorporate detoxifying foods and drinks into your routine, such as fresh fruits and vegetables, herbal teas, and water infused with lemon and cucumber. Lastly, getting enough sleep is crucial for your overall health and well-being. Lack of sleep can affect your mood, concentration, and even your physical health. Aim for at least 7-8 hours of sleep each night to ensure that you are well-rested and energized for the day ahead.

In conclusion, incorporating these self-care practices into your routine can help you become the healthiest version of yourself, both physically and mentally, and ultimately allow you to take better care of those around you. It is ultimately up to you to choose your own self-care regime: teas, supplements, foods, exercise, books, arts, hydration. trusting your intuition is a process worth all of the effort you give to it.

Simple steps to incorporate guided imagery and visualization techniques into your daily routine:

1. Find a quiet and comfortable place where you won't be disturbed for a few minutes.
2. Close your eyes and take a few deep breaths to help you relax.
3. Choose a mental image or positive outcome to focus on. This could be a peaceful scene like a beach or a forest or a positive outcome like acing an exam or succeeding in a job interview.
4. Visualize this image or outcome in as much detail as possible. Use all your senses to create a vivid mental picture of the scene or experience.
5. Focus on the positive emotions associated with this image or outcome. Imagine how it would feel to be in that peaceful environment or to experience that positive outcome.
6. Stay with this image or outcome for a few minutes, continuing to breathe deeply and focusing on the positive emotions it brings up.
7. When you're ready, slowly open your eyes and take a few deep breaths before returning to your day.

Chapter 3: Mental Health for Moms

Envision yourself suddenly being solely responsible for a child or two, earning perhaps $25,000 to $30,000 annually, witnessing your friends gradually drifting away, and constantly feeling scrutinized for your parenting abilities, eventually struggling with negative thoughts regardless of how hard you are trying to handle the situation at your best.

Welcome to the everyday reality of a typical single mother.

Being a single mother demands an extraordinary amount of strength and resilience. With the absence of a partner or co-parent to share the burdens and responsibilities, you carry the weight of the world on your shoulders. It is impossible to ignore the fact that raising a child alone poses twice the challenge for women, and the pressure can become overwhelming because of the intrusive thoughts that provoke anxiety. This pressure intensifies when you bear the sole responsibility of caring for your child, along with managing finances and providing not only for their physical needs but also their emotional well-being while juggling your physical and mental health, work, social life, and personal space. As you endeavor to strike a balance between all these, regardless of how much you have on your plate, stressors accumulate, and they can escalate into a mental health crisis and may lead to poor well-being.

Intrusive thoughts are unwelcomed and involuntary thoughts, images, or impulses that repeatedly enter your mind, causing you distress or anxiety. These thoughts are typically disturbing, bizarre, or taboo in nature, often centering around themes such as violence, harm, sexual content, irrational fears, or feelings of inadequacy. These thoughts can be vivid and intense, creating a sense of discomfort and unease for you. The relentless presence of intrusive thoughts creates a constant state of tension, fear, and anxiety for single moms like you. Your minds become flooded with disturbing and unwanted images, ideas, or consequences, which can be both emotionally and mentally draining. The weight of these intrusive thoughts adds to the already heavy load of responsibilities you carry, making it difficult to find respite or peace of mind.

Research indicates that single mothers face an increased likelihood of experiencing psychological issues, such as mood disorders, major depressive disorder, and generalized anxiety disorder. [34] Moreover, the added concern of not being able to meet their children's needs adequately further compounds the stress in an already demanding situation, potentially exacerbating the mental health conditions of these mothers. To understand how this process works, let us have a look at this single mother named Christine. She is trying to figure out how to pay the bills and provide for her children with the limited income she earns. Because of her limited resource and past unfortunate experiences, she begins having intrusive thoughts of losing her job and becoming homeless. Constant threats from the landlord aggravate her thoughts as she imagines herself and her children being thrown out of the house, living on the streets, and facing hunger and despair. Despite her efforts to focus on finding solutions and remaining positive, or even seeking help, these intrusive thought keeps intruding into her mind, causing anxiety and adding to the already overwhelming stress she experiences daily.

---

[3] Subramaniam, M., Prasad, R. O., Abdin, E., Vaingankar, J. A., & Chong, S. A. (2014). Single mothers have a higher risk of mood disorders. Annals of the Academy of Medicine, Singapore, 43(3), 145–151.

[4] Nahar, J. S., Algin, S., Sajib, M. W. H., Ahmed, S., & Arafat, S. M. Y. (2020). Depressive and anxiety disorders among single mothers in Dhaka. International Journal of Social Psychiatry, 66(5), 485-488. doi:10.1177/0020764020920671.

Like Christine, in addition to the practical and financial aspects, you may often find yourself feeling isolated and lonely, which keeps you from reaching out to potential support networks for help. Where your attention and thoughts should be focused on moving on, accepting reality, and problem-solving, these intrusive thoughts may constantly take you back to feelings of resentment and the unfortunate incidents that led you to where you are at the moment, making you feel even more lonely. The more you try to rebuke these thoughts, the more they seem to overtake you. As a consequence, you can regress in your development and feel emotionally drained to the extent that you feel like giving up on almost everything.

Let us have a look at the way these thoughts work to diminish your motivation, impact your actions and hinder your progress.

1. **Motivation:** Intrusive thoughts can diminish your motivation by occupying your mind with negative or distressing content. Constantly battling these thoughts drains your mental and emotional energy, making it challenging to find the drive and enthusiasm to pursue your goals. The intrusive thoughts may create doubts, fears, or feelings of

inadequacy, dampening your motivation to take action and move forward.

For instance: Emily is a single mother who works two jobs to provide for her child. Despite facing financial struggles and limited time, she is determined to create a better life for her family. However, intrusive thoughts significantly affect her motivation.

Every time Emily sits down to make a budget or set financial goals, intrusive thoughts flood her mind. She begins to doubt her ability to make ends meet, fearing that she will not be able to provide enough for her child's needs. Thoughts of being judged by others and feeling like a failure as a parent intensify her feelings of overwhelm.

As a result, Emily's motivation takes a hit. The self-doubt and fears generated by intrusive thoughts drain her energy and enthusiasm. She finds it challenging to maintain the drive to work long hours and make sacrifices for her family. The constant mental and emotional burden makes her question whether her efforts are worth it, leading to a decline in motivation.

2. **Actions:** Intrusive thoughts can hinder your actions by causing self-doubt and hesitation. When intrusive thoughts fill your mind, you may second-guess yourself or fear the potential consequences of your actions. This can lead to procrastination, avoidance, or reluctance to take risks. As a result, your progress may be impeded as you struggle to initiate or follow through with the necessary actions.

   For example, Michelle is a single mother who works full-time to support her family. She has been considering going back to school to pursue a higher degree, as she believes it would provide better opportunities for her and her children in the long run. However, she often experiences intrusive thoughts that hinder her actions. Whenever Michelle thinks about enrolling in classes, intrusive thoughts flood her mind, causing self-doubt and hesitation. She starts to worry about the potential consequences of her decision: Will she be able to balance work, parenting, and studying? What if she fails or can't keep up with the coursework? These thoughts fill her with fear and uncertainty.

   As a result of these intrusive thoughts, Michelle finds herself second-guessing her abilities and delaying taking action. She starts procrastinating on researching schools or applying for programs. She becomes hesitant to take the necessary steps to initiate the enrollment process, constantly questioning whether she is making the right decision for herself and her children.

Michelle's progress toward pursuing her education is impeded due to the intrusive thoughts. She avoids confronting her fears and taking risks, which prevents her from moving forward with her goals. Despite recognizing the potential benefits of furthering her education, she finds herself trapped in a cycle of self-doubt and hesitation, unable to take the necessary actions to make progress.

Take a moment to reflect: Do you find yourself caught in a similar pattern of intrusive thoughts hindering your actions?

3. **Progress:** Intrusive thoughts can disrupt your progress by diverting your attention and focus away from your goals. Instead of devoting your mental resources to problem-solving and moving forward, you may find yourself trapped in a cycle of rumination and overthinking, analyzing the intrusive thoughts and their meaning. This preoccupation

hampers your ability to make meaningful strides toward your objectives, potentially causing delays or stagnation in your progress.

To Illustrate: Rachel is a single mother who has been working on her fitness goals. She wants to improve her health, lose weight, and set a positive example for her children. However, intrusive thoughts disrupt her progress.

Whenever Rachel starts her workout routine or plans her meals, intrusive thoughts flood her mind. She finds herself constantly questioning her abilities and doubting her potential for success. Thoughts like "What if I can't stick to this?" or "Am I doing enough?" consume her thoughts and cause her to second-guess herself. Instead of devoting her mental resources to her fitness goals, Rachel gets trapped in a cycle of rumination. She spends excessive time analyzing intrusive thoughts and worrying about potential obstacles and setbacks. This preoccupation diverts her attention away from taking consistent actions toward her objectives.

As a result, Rachel's progress in achieving her fitness goals is disrupted. The time and energy she could have dedicated to working out or meal planning are spent on overthinking and analyzing intrusive thoughts. She finds herself procrastinating on her workouts or making unhealthy food choices due to the self-doubt and hesitation caused by intrusive thoughts. This delay and lack of consistent action hinder her progress, making it harder for her to achieve the desired results.

It is crucial to address these intrusive thoughts before they overwhelm your mind and drain the energy you need to nurture a happy and healthy family. Recognize that if left unattended, these thoughts can become ingrained patterns that unconsciously influence your behavior. Taking proactive steps to confront and manage them is essential for your well-being and the well-being of your family.

Learning to differentiate between rational and irrational thoughts can indeed be an effective way to deal with intrusive thoughts. By recognizing and challenging irrational thoughts, you can gain a better understanding of their validity and reduce their impact. Here is how you can go about addressing and getting rid of intrusive thoughts with the categorization of rational and irrational thinking:

Step 1: Identify irrational thoughts:

Begin by becoming aware of the intrusive thoughts that are causing distress or anxiety. Take note of the specific content and patterns of these thoughts.

Step 2: Question the evidence:

Examine the evidence supporting these thoughts. Ask yourself if there is any concrete proof or logical reasoning behind them. Often, intrusive thoughts are based on fears, assumptions, or distorted perceptions rather than actual evidence.

Step 3: Challenge irrational thoughts:

Engage in rational thinking by actively challenging irrational thoughts. Ask yourself if there are alternative explanations or more realistic perspectives that can counter these intrusive thoughts. Look for evidence that contradicts or weakens their validity.

Step 4: Replace with rational thoughts:

Replace irrational thoughts with rational ones that are based on logic and evidence. Focus on realistic and positive interpretations of situations. Practice affirmations or positive self-talk to reinforce more rational thinking patterns.

Step 5: Seek external perspectives:

Talk to trusted friends, family, or a mental health professional about your intrusive thoughts. They can provide objective viewpoints and help you identify irrational thinking patterns that you may not have noticed on your own.

Step 6: Practice cognitive-behavioral techniques:
Cognitive-behavioral therapy (CBT) techniques can be particularly helpful in addressing irrational thinking. These techniques involve identifying cognitive distortions, challenging negative thoughts, and replacing them with more rational and balanced ones.

Step 7: Practice self-compassion:
Be kind and compassionate towards yourself when dealing with intrusive thoughts. Understand that these thoughts are not a reflection of your worth or abilities as a mother. Treat yourself with patience, understanding, and self-care as you navigate this process.

Now let us go through this strategy once again with the example of Hannah, who had recurrent thoughts about financial concerns. You will see how she practiced this approach and gradually learned to differentiate between rational and irrational thinking, breaking the pattern of harmful thoughts that took a toll on her mental health, causing anxiety and distress. These steps empowered her to focus on the broader aspects of parenting and finding alternative ways to provide for her child's well-being beyond financial resources.

1. **Identify irrational thoughts:** Hannah, a single mother, frequently experiences intrusive thoughts that she is not providing enough for her child financially. This thought often arises when she sees other families with more financial resources or when she struggles to make ends meet.

2. **Question the evidence:** She examines the evidence supporting the thought that she is not providing enough financially. She realizes that she is working hard to meet her child's basic needs and has made sacrifices to ensure their well-being. She acknowledges that comparing herself to others or society's expectations may not be a fair or accurate measure of her abilities as a provider.

3. **Challenge irrational thoughts:** Hannah actively began to challenge irrational thoughts by questioning their validity. She asks herself if there are alternative ways to define what it means to provide for her child. She recognizes that financial security is just one

aspect of parenting and that emotional support, love, and nurturing are equally important, which is able to meet well.

4. **Replace with rational thoughts:** Consequently, she replaces irrational thoughts with rational ones. Instead of focusing solely on financial resources, she emphasizes the love, care, and stability she provides for her child. She acknowledges that she is doing her best given her circumstances and that her child's well-being extends beyond monetary measures.

5. **Seek external perspectives:** She also seeks advice from a financial counselor who specializes in assisting single parents. The counselor helps her develop a budgeting plan, explore available resources, and gain a better understanding of how she can optimize her financial situation. This external perspective reassures her that she is taking proactive steps to provide for her child.

6. **Practice cognitive-behavioral techniques:** She practices cognitive-behavioral techniques by challenging negative thoughts whenever they arise. When intrusive thoughts about not providing financially enough emerge, she counters them with

rational and positive affirmations about her efforts as a single mother.

7. **Practice self-compassion:** Throughout this process, the single mother practices self-compassion. She reminds herself that financial challenges are common and that she is not alone in facing them. She treats herself with kindness, acknowledging that she is doing the best she can in her unique circumstances.

By applying these strategies to Hannah's feelings of financial inadequacy, she gradually learns to differentiate between rational and irrational thinking. This empowers her to focus on the broader aspects of parenting and find alternative ways to provide for her child's well-being beyond financial resources. By doing so, she not only aims to do good for her child/ren but also creates an understanding space, which is crucial for her mental health and well-being.

This understanding exhibited towards others in your life, and especially towards yourself first, is known as empathy. Empathy is the ability to understand and share the feelings, experiences, and perspectives of others. It involves putting oneself in someone else's shoes, seeing the world through their eyes, and connecting with their emotions. Empathy goes beyond sympathy, which is merely acknowledging someone's feelings. Instead, empathy requires actively experiencing and comprehending another person's emotions, allowing for a deeper level of understanding and connection. It involves being sensitive to the needs and struggles of others and responding with kindness, compassion, and support. Empathy is a fundamental aspect of human connection, fostering understanding, communication, and the cultivation of meaningful relationships.

Building on the same foundation, we have empathetic living that takes empathy a step further by incorporating it into one's daily life and mindset. It is one of the key ingredients in healthy single motherhood is embracing empathetic living. Empathetic living means nurturing a mindset of understanding, compassion, and empathy towards both yourself and others surrounding you because it helps you to tone down the excessive toll you take on yourself and your health in the name of perfection and self-criticism. Simply put, empathetic living is intentions and thoughts put into action.

Let us have a look at two different examples of empathetic living towards yourself and your child. Through the following example, you can see how you can develop a mindset that will lead you to a more content life. Since charity begins at home, I will start with the example that focuses on you first.

Sophia is a single mother who practices empathetic living in her relationship with herself.

1. **Self-Compassion:** Sophia acknowledges the challenges and demands she faces as a single mother. She recognizes that she is doing the best she can with the resources and support available to her. Instead of being hard on herself for any perceived shortcomings or mistakes, Sophia practices self-compassion. She treats herself with kindness, understanding, and forgiveness, embracing the truth that she is a human being with limitations and deserves love and care as much as other mothers out there.

2. **Self-Care:** Sophia prioritizes her own well-being and self-care. She understands that taking care of herself is essential for being a present and healthy parent. She makes sure to set aside time for activities that bring her joy and relaxation, whether it is reading a book, practicing yoga, or engaging in a hobby. She nurtures her physical, emotional, and mental health, ensuring she has the energy and resilience to face the challenges of single motherhood. She understands that a dry well cannot quench the thirst.

3. **Boundaries and Balance:** Sophia sets boundaries to protect her time, energy, and emotional well-being. She recognizes that it is okay to say no to excessive commitments or demands that may overwhelm her. Sophia creates a healthy balance between her responsibilities as a parent and her own personal needs, understanding that she deserves time for self-reflection, personal growth, and pursuing her passions. Some things can always wait.

4. **Positive Self-Talk:** Sophia cultivates a positive and empowering inner dialogue. She consciously replaces self-critical thoughts with self-affirming and compassionate thoughts. She reminds herself of her strengths, resilience, and the love she provides for her child/ren. She remembers to celebrate her accomplishments, no matter how small, and acknowledges her efforts as a single mother.

5. **Seeking Support:** Sophia understands the importance of seeking support from others. She connects with fellow single mothers, close family members, or friends, engages in support groups, or seeks therapy if needed. She recognizes that she does not have to face the challenges alone and that

reaching out for help is a sign of strength, not weakness.

By practicing empathetic living towards herself and cultivating self-compassion, self-care, boundaries, positive self-talk, and seeking support when needed, Sophia enables herself to maintain her well-being and find fulfillment in her personal life.

Now moving on to the example of empathetic living towards your child. Let us continue with the example of Sophia, who is raising her teenage daughter, Maya. Sophia practices empathetic living in her relationship with Maya.

1. **Understanding and Validation:** Sophia recognizes the challenges that Maya faces as a teenager growing up in a single-parent household. She acknowledges the various emotions Maya experiences, such as frustration, loneliness, or a desire for more family support, particularly from a father. Sophia actively listens to Maya's concerns, providing a safe space for her to express herself without judgment. Note that Sophia does not belittle or dismiss her daughter's emotions with statements like "There are several other kids in the world who are living with a single parent, and then there are even those who do not even

have one parent." She validates Maya's feelings, letting her know that her emotions are valid and understandable given the circumstances.

2. **Empathy in Decision-Making:** Sophia takes Maya's perspective into consideration when making decisions that affect both of them. She understands that Maya may have unique needs and desires as a teenager, and she strives to balance those with their overall well-being. Sophia involves Maya in discussions about important family matters and values her input, making her feel heard and respected.

3. **Support and Nurturing:** Sophia offers unwavering support and nurturing to Maya. She takes the time to understand Maya's interests, passions, and goals and encourages her to pursue them. Sophia attends Maya's extracurricular activities, shows genuine interest in her hobbies, and provides guidance when Maya faces challenges. Sophia's empathetic approach helps Maya feel loved, valued, and understood, promoting a strong bond between them. Sophia also understands that there may be times when she will have her own commitments and may not be able to always participate in Maya's interests

or extracurricular activities. Along with practicing empathetic living towards her daughter Sophia does not lose the hem of empathetic living towards herself.

4. **Teaching Empathy:** Sophia actively teaches Maya the value of empathy and the importance of understanding and caring for others. She encourages Maya to develop an understanding and compassionate behavior toward her peers, family members, and those in need. Sophia leads by example, demonstrating acts of kindness and compassion in their daily interactions and teaching Maya the importance of putting herself in others' shoes.

By practicing empathetic living towards her child, Sophia creates a nurturing and supportive environment where Maya feels understood, accepted, and loved. This empathetic approach strengthens their mother-daughter relationship, fostering open communication and a deep sense of connection.

In the end, as you reflect on the journey of single motherhood, maintaining mental health, practicing empathetic living, and implementing various techniques to reduce stress and anxiety, it is essential to recognize the profound importance of time to time assessing your personal growth and development. Do not forget to take a moment for self-reflection and check in with yourself. Assess where you currently stand on your journey and how far you have come. Think about how you are feeling about it; it is always good to write things down.

Pause and ask yourself: How am I really doing? Are there any areas of my life that require attention and nurturing? Are there any self-limiting beliefs or negative patterns of thinking that are holding me back? If so, what do I need to do about it other than what I am already doing?

Lastly, learn the art and joy of being grateful and living in the present through practicing mindfulness over mind fullness. Mindfulness invites you to cultivate a deep awareness of the present moment, embracing it with openness and non-judgment.

In the midst of the many responsibilities and challenges you face, it is easy to become overwhelmed and lose yourself in a state of mind full of anything and everything around you. The constant stream of thoughts, worries, and distractions can cloud your ability to fully engage with the present and savor the precious moments with your children.

By choosing mindfulness, you tap into your inner

wellspring of peace and clarity, which also promotes your mental health. Mindfulness allows you to bring your full attention to the present, embracing each experience with a sense of curiosity and gratitude. It grants you the power to consciously choose your thoughts and reactions rather than being swept away by the chaos of daily life. Through mindfulness, you can discover moments of calm amidst the storm. It enables you to be fully present with your children, truly listening to their words and cherishing the connections you share. Mindfulness also nurtures your own well-being, providing a sanctuary of self-care and self-compassion.

Every single day, gift yourself with a precious moment of deep, intentional breathing, anchoring yourself in the present moment. Embrace a gentle awareness of your thoughts, emotions, and sensations, extending kindness and understanding to yourself. Through the practice of mindfulness, you will witness the gradual fading away of the noise and distractions that often consume your mind. In their place, you will discover an inner sanctuary of peace and equilibrium, where a profound sense of serenity resides. It is within this space that you unlock the transformative power of mindfulness, enabling you to navigate the complexities of life with grace and resilience. In those moments of stillness and presence, you connect with your innate wisdom, accessing a wellspring of strength and clarity. As you cultivate this practice, you not only cultivate your own well-being but also create a haven of tranquility for yourself and your precious children. Remember, by prioritizing mindfulness, you gift yourself the tools to embrace each day with calmness, find balance amidst the chaos, and foster an environment of peace and love.

Chapter 4: Recreating Meaning

As you turn the page to a new chapter, dear single mother, you enter the door of recreating meaning in your life. You have endured the tough times and weathered your share of suffering, facing those heavy nights with strength and resilience. There have been moments when you took the time to reflect and perhaps even lament over the decisions you made, whether they were made willingly or imposed upon you. Now is the moment to release all those resentments, to free yourself from the burden of "why me," and to stop yearning for a return to the past. Instead, embrace the realization that you have already weathered the storm with unwavering determination, dealing with tough times that may have taken a toll on your health and mental well-being. Choose to let go of the weight of the past and set your sights on a new beginning. Trust in your ability to create a life that reflects the strength and courage you've shown as a single mother. Every step you take, fueled by the lessons learned and the growth experienced, brings you closer to a life filled with happiness, fulfillment, and peace.

Undoubtedly, creating a life you and your children

can be proud of is a challenging endeavor, requiring significant effort in both theory and practice. However, challenges does not equate to impossible. In fact, with the right guidance and determination, you can achieve this transformation. Allow me to share valuable tips and secret ingredients that will pave the way for a productive and flourishing life. These essential insights will unfold in the following chapters, offering you a roadmap toward personal growth and fulfillment. Embrace this journey with optimism, knowing that each step you take brings you closer to a life filled with pride, contentment, and success for yourself and your children.

Let's start by taking a moment to reflect on your journey, dear single mother. Consider how far you've come from where you once were and where you stand today. It's natural to feel that there's still a long road ahead, and indeed, there may be. However, do not lose hope or become disheartened. I assure you that with unwavering perseverance and dedication, nothing can hinder your progress. Remember the wisdom in the saying, *"In all toil, there is profit, but mere talk leads only to poverty."* Embrace the value of hard work and action, for it is through your persistent efforts that you will find the rewards you seek.

Pause and reflect on your experiences and growth.

Consider the changes you've made and those you wish to make. Embrace the notion that true transformation starts from within, and preparing your mind and heart is the key to conquering the challenges ahead.

Imagine this chapter as a blank canvas, ready for your unique masterpiece. You have recognized the areas in your life that need a makeover, and you have mustered the courage to confront the challenges that held you back. Now, it's time to take practical actions that will propel you toward a life filled with purpose, fulfillment, and joy. Begin by envisioning the life you want to create for yourself and your children. What does it look like? How does it feel?

For example, you may envision creating a home where open communication and mutual respect thrive. Picture yourself engaging in meaningful conversations with your children, where their thoughts and feelings are valued. Envision setting aside quality time for shared activities that promote bonding and create lasting memories. Cultivating joy and living a contented life becomes an essential focus as you continue on your journey of recreating meaning. It is a deliberate choice to prioritize happiness and seek moments of joy amidst the daily responsibilities and challenges you face.

Additionally, imagine yourself pursuing your

passions and interests. Picture the fulfillment that comes from pursuing a career or educational path that aligns with your values and aspirations. Envision the joy and satisfaction of achieving personal milestones and setting an example of perseverance and ambition for your children.

Now, allow your dreams and aspirations to guide you as you embark on this next phase. Remember, dear single mother, and you possess the power to shape your own destiny and redefine what things mean to you. Maybe there was a time when quality time meant having a cozy dinner with your partner and being physically intimate, but now taking your kids out in the park and playing with them is the definition of quality time. Similarly, there may be several other things with meaning you would have to recreate to get yourself out of the whirlwind of resentments. Weekends are yet another example where you used to explore new places and restaurants with your partner or maybe go have a romantic dinner with him, but now weekends become an opportunity to engage in fun and meaningful experiences with your child. Whether it's exploring local parks, visiting children's museums, or embarking on little adventures together, every weekend holds the potential for creating cherished memories as a single mother.

Value of Small Steps:

All of this is not going to be accomplished in one night. You know that well, right? Therefore, embrace the notion that small steps can lead to significant changes. Break down your goals into manageable actions and take consistent strides toward them. Whether it's pursuing further education, exploring new career opportunities, or cultivating healthier relationships, each step you take brings you closer to the life you envision.

There may be obstacles and setbacks along the way. If there comes a moment when you have run out of strength and motivation, do not be ashamed to seek support from your loved ones and surround yourself with individuals who uplift and inspire you. Connect with other single mothers who are also on a path of personal growth. Share experiences, exchange ideas, and celebrate one another's victories. Together, you can create a network of encouragement and empowerment that propels you forward.

Be the Hero of Your Life:

As a single mother, it is natural to experience moments of vulnerability and longing for support, especially when facing the challenges of parenthood alone. Embrace your vulnerability as a single mother (until you find the right partner again), but remember not to allow it to pull you back to your ex-partner. Instead, redefine what it means to be a hero in your and your child's life by taking charge and rewriting your story. However, in rewriting your story as the hero of your life, it's crucial to recognize the immense strength and resilience within you, independent of anyone else's presence.

Embrace your new role with courage and determination, focusing on building a fulfilling and empowered life for yourself and your children. You possess the power to provide the love, care, and support your family needs, and you have the inner resources to overcome challenges with grace; it is just that you have to gradually work towards managing things in your life and get accustomed to these new feelings and routines. Reframe your perspective by valuing yourself as an individual with adequate worth. Your value isn't defined by external relationships but by the strength and love you bring to your role as a single mother.

Remember, being the hero of your life entails taking charge of your narrative and creating a path aligned with your goals and aspirations. Trust in your abilities and believe in the power of your love and dedication to guide your family toward a fulfilling and joyful life. And while you may experience moments of sadness or longing, let those emotions fuel your determination to thrive and succeed. As the hero of your life, you possess the strength to face challenges, the wisdom to learn from experiences, and the ability to create a life that reflects your values and dreams.

Embrace this new chapter with hope and optimism, knowing that you hold the pen to your story rewriting it with resilience, self-compassion, and the understanding that you can craft a beautiful and meaningful life for yourself and your children, filled with love, joy, and endless possibilities.

The Power of Gratitude:

No matter how challenging the early days have been and how different life may be from your expectations. As a single mother, never underestimate the power of gratitude, for it aligns beautifully with the Law of Attraction. Embrace gratitude as a daily practice and instill it in your children's lives as well. By doing so, you open the door to attracting more positive experiences and abundance into your life. The Law of Attraction states that like attracts like, so when you focus on the blessings and positive aspects of your life, you attract more of the same.

When you take time each day to reflect on the blessings in your life and appreciate the love and bond you share with your children, you are setting a powerful intention to attract more love and joy into your life. Your gratitude acts as a magnet, drawing in more heartwarming moments and deeper connections with your children. As you express gratitude for the precious time spent with them, the universe responds by bringing forth even more opportunities for quality moments of love and laughter.

Moreover, as you acknowledge the challenges you have faced and the strength that helped you overcome them, you are affirming your resilience and determination. This positive mindset sends a signal to the universe that you are capable of overcoming obstacles and are ready for more opportunities for growth and success. The Law of Attraction responds to this empowering energy by bringing forth circumstances and opportunities that further fuel your growth and success.

Expressing gratitude for the support systems and individuals who have shown kindness and offered assistance along your journey is also important. Recognize the friends, family members, or community organizations that have provided emotional support, practical help, or a listening ear during times of need. Show appreciation for their presence and contributions to your life. When you show appreciation for the people who have been there for you, you attract more positive and supportive relationships into your life. Your gratitude creates a harmonious flow of kindness and support, inviting even more loving and supportive people to enter your life's journey. Embrace gratitude for everything you can see, feel, and experience, including the challenges you have faced, like the separation from your partner. Looking back, you realize that this experience has brought out the best in you and taught you valuable lessons. It reminds you that being alone is far better than being with a partner who couldn't fully be there for you even in fundamental aspects let alone every aspect. Gratitude allows you to see the silver linings in all situations, opening your heart to more positivity and growth. By cultivating gratitude for the opportunities and resources available to you, you are magnetizing more possibilities and abundance. Embracing a sense of gratitude for the future and the ability to create a fulfilling life for yourself and your children sets a powerful intention for attracting even more blessings and opportunities. The Law of Attraction responds by aligning you with opportunities and resources that resonate with your positive intentions.

Remember, the Law of Attraction responds to the energy you emit into the world. When you practice gratitude and focus on the positive aspects of your life, you raise your vibrational frequency, making it easier to attract more positive experiences. Embrace gratitude as a potent tool to enrich your relationship with yourself, your children, and the world around you, and watch as the Law of Attraction responds to your positive energy, bringing forth even greater blessings and opportunities. Your journey as a single mother is an incredible manifestation of strength, love, and abundance, and with gratitude as your guiding light, the universe conspires to support you every step of the way.

Above all, live in peace and find joy in the things you do. Nurture your passions and interests, no matter how small or seemingly insignificant they may be. Engage in activities that bring you joy, whether it's pursuing a hobby, discovering new talents, or dedicating time to self-care. Embrace moments of creativity, laughter, and playfulness, allowing yourself to fully indulge in the joy they bring.

Surround yourself with a supportive community that uplifts and inspires you. Connect with like-minded individuals who share similar passions and values. Seek positive role models who can guide and mentor you on your path. Together, you can create a network of encouragement and celebration, amplifying the joy in your life. Practice mindfulness and be fully present in each moment. Take notice of the simple pleasures that often go unnoticed, such as:

- **Sunrise and sunset:** Witnessing the beauty of the sun rising and setting can be a breathtaking experience, reminding us of the beauty of nature and the passing of time.

- **A warm cup of tea or coffee:** Savoring a hot beverage can bring comfort and a moment of relaxation amid a busy day.
- **Laughing with loved ones:** Sharing a genuine laugh with family or friends can uplift your spirits and strengthen bonds.
- **Hugs from your children:** Embrace the warmth and love in a hug from your child, feeling the connection between you both.
- **Listening to your favorite song:** Music has the power to evoke emotions and memories, bringing joy and comfort.
- **A walk in nature:** Strolling through a park, forest, or beach can be rejuvenating and grounding.
- **A good book or movie:** Getting lost in a captivating story can provide an escape and a chance to unwind.
- **Cooking a delicious meal:** Preparing and enjoying a homemade meal can be a gratifying experience.
- **Feeling the warmth of sunlight on your skin:** Basking in the sunshine can lift your mood and make you feel more connected to the world.

- **Watching children play:** Observing the innocence and joy of children at play can bring a smile to your face.

- **A phone call from a friend or family member:** Receiving a call from someone you care about can brighten your day and remind you of the importance of connections.

- **Petting a furry friend:** Interacting with pets can reduce stress and provide a sense of companionship and love.

- **Acts of kindness:** Witnessing or experiencing acts of kindness can restore faith in humanity and inspire you to do the same for others.

- **A moment of silence and stillness:** Taking a pause from the busyness of life to enjoy quiet moments of reflection and relaxation.

There is so much more to find joy in and to be grateful for. You just have to let go of comparisons and societal expectations, and definitions that are overrated. Create your own meaning, peace, and joy while walking your own unique journey. Recognize that true contentment comes from aligning your life with your values and aspirations rather than conforming to external standards. Embrace self-acceptance and celebrate your accomplishments, no matter how small they may seem.

Last but not least, prioritize self-care and self-compassion. Recognize that you deserve love, care, and nurturing just as much as your children do. Set aside time for activities that recharge and replenish you. Practice self-compassion by offering yourself kindness, understanding, and forgiveness. Remember, you are worthy of joy and contentment.

Dear single mother, as you cultivate joy and embrace a contented life, you create a ripple effect of positivity in the lives of your children and those around you. By prioritizing happiness, nurturing your passions, and surrounding yourself with positivity, you set a powerful example for your children to lead joyful lives.

So, dear single mother, let joy be your guiding light on this journey of recreating meaning. Embrace the beauty in each day, celebrate your accomplishments, and cherish the moments of joy that come your way. By living a contentment-filled life, you create a legacy of resilience, happiness, and fulfillment that will inspire generations to come.

Chapter 5: Intuitive Goal Setting

Intuition is a fascinating aspect of the human mind that has been the subject of much discussion and debate throughout history. The mysterious force guides you when you are faced with difficult decisions, the quiet voice that warns you when something is not quite right, and the source of your deepest insights and inspirations. From the ancient Greeks who believed in the power of their oracles to the modern-day entrepreneurs who rely on their gut instincts to make game-changing decisions, intuition has been a driving force behind some of humanity's greatest achievements. So, what is intuition, and how can you learn to harness its power to make better decisions and live more fulfilling lives?

Intuition is the ability to understand or perceive something immediately without conscious reasoning. It is often described as a "gut feeling" or an inner voice that guides your thoughts and actions. It is believed to be a combination of your past experiences, knowledge, and predominantly subconscious processes, which allow you to quickly make decisions and judgments. Learning to rely on your intuition can be important in various aspects of your life, as it can help you make better decisions, especially in situations where you may not have all the information or time to analyze a situation thoroughly.

For example, when you meet someone for the first time, an example of intuition could be the feeling that you get. Even if you don't have any logical or tangible reasons to justify it, you may feel uneasy or uncomfortable around them or feel an instant connection and warmth toward them. People often refer to this feeling as a "gut feeling" or a "hunch," and it is believed to be the result of subconscious processes in the brain that analyze and interpret subtle cues such as body language, tone of voice, and facial expressions. Your intuition may guide your decision to pursue or avoid a relationship or interaction with that person, and it may turn out to be a valuable guide for future interactions with them.

Or, if you're considering a career change, you might have made a list of pros and cons and done extensive research on different options, but you may still feel uncertain about which path to take. In this situation, you might experience a feeling in your gut that one option feels right, even if it doesn't seem to be the most practical or logical choice.

In this scenario, trusting your intuition could lead to positive growth, milestone achievements, and the accomplishment of your goals that you may not have achieved if you played it safe or made a more conventional choice. Following your intuition can help you stay true to yourself and your values and can guide you toward opportunities for personal and professional growth that you may not have considered otherwise. It can also help you navigate challenges and setbacks along the way, as you're more likely to stay motivated and committed to your goals if you're doing work that feels meaningful and authentic to you.

However, this is not always the case. Trusting your intuition can sometimes lead you to negative outcomes, but that doesn't mean you should always ignore it. Instead, you can strike a balance by using your intuition as one of several tools in your decision-making process instead of blindly trusting your intuition and making it the sole basis of taking a significant step in your life. You may take a calculated risk that is seconded by intuition, and for that, you must combine your intuition with logical analysis and data-driven decision-making. This means that you should listen to your intuition and take it into account, but also do your research and gather all the relevant information to make an informed decision. You can also seek the advice and feedback of trusted friends, family members, or colleagues, as they can provide you with valuable insights and perspectives.

It is also essential to consider the situation's context. Intuition may be more valuable in social situations, while logic may be more helpful with objective data. Practicing self-awareness, reflecting on past experiences, and analyzing outcomes can help you recognize when to use intuition and how to combine it with logical analysis for better decision-making. Trusting your inner voice can be invaluable when it comes to making important decisions. While intuition may not always be loud, it can be accessed through mindfulness or meditation practices, along with journaling. It's important to be aware that your ego or inner critic may also arise and may be louder due to familiarity. However, with practice, patience, and time, you can tune into your intuition and unlock its power. It's important to remember that intuition is a natural part of who you are, waiting for you to listen and trust its guidance.

At times, it can be challenging to balance the practical demands of decision-making with the emotional aspects of promoting self-love and positivity. It's important to recognize that these two approaches are not mutually exclusive but can instead complement each other. When you trust your intuition and listen to your inner voice, you are better equipped to make decisions that align with your values and goals while also promoting self-love and personal growth. By integrating logical analysis and emotional awareness, you can make decisions that honor your practical needs and your emotional well-being.

Promoting love and self-love is powerful, with the potential to transform lives and empower you to achieve your goals and fulfill their potential. By cultivating a deep and abiding love for oneself, you create a foundation of self-worth and self-respect that can inspire you to push beyond your perceived limits and accomplish greater things. Whether your goals are short-term or long-term, you can benefit from a mindset of positivity, growth, and self-love that encourages you to take risks, overcome obstacles, and celebrate your successes along the way. By supporting one another in this journey and fostering a community of love and respect, you can create a world in which everyone has the opportunity to thrive and achieve their dreams.

Let no one tell you that you do not have the power to transform your life or achieve your goals and dreams. I must tell you that through the practice of self-love, it is doable. When you cultivate a deep sense of love and respect for yourself, you develop a strong foundation of self-worth and self-confidence that enables you to push beyond your perceived limits and take risks that lead to growth and achievement. I am not saying that you must make unrealistic goals after reading that you have the power to change lives and realize your dreams. Instead, what I am trying to foster is that you can eradicate the negative energies and put aside the mean things that others say about you and focus on what God truly has in store for you. See yourself with God's eyes so that you can love yourself the way He loves you.

It is important to note that with self-love (God's love actualized), you can better navigate obstacles, persevere through challenges, and celebrate your successes, all of which contribute to positive growth and forward momentum in your life. God sees us as His precious children and loves us above all things. If it wasn't so, He would not have sacrificed His Son for our ransom. In the book of Isaiah, God says, *"Since you are precious and honored in my sight and because I love you, I will give people in exchange for you,"* and in the gospel of Mathew chapter 10, Christ made it evident that we are dearer to Him than any other living being when He said, *"Fear not, therefore; you are of more value than many sparrows."* Therefore, do not think of yourself as anything less because the Creator of the Universe loves you to bits, and you must see yourself and others the same way He sees and values you to achieve greater things in life

Ultimately, self-love is a key ingredient in the recipe

for success and fulfillment and can help you live your best life. It doesn't mean that you have to flip your entire life after this notion and begin screeching about all day long. Instead, you can incorporate minor efforts into your daily routine to establish a behavior full of self-love.

A routine that incorporates and promotes self-love that can be achieved through a daily routine prioritizing self-care and positive self-talk may look like this:

Morning routine:

- Waking early with the intention to practice gratitude in prayer or meditation.
- Hydrating with water. Exercising vigorously for 5-15 minutes.
- Stretching can set a positive tone for the day.
- Engaging in activities that bring joy, such as listening to music or reading, uplifts one's mood.

Mid-Day routine:

- Throughout the day, take breaks to breathe deeply.
- Checking in with one's emotions can provide a sense of mindfulness and self-awareness.
- Practicing positive self-talk and affirmations, such as reciting daily mantras or writing down positive thoughts, to cultivate a sense of self-love and self-worth.

Evening and bed-time routine:

- Prioritizing rest and relaxation in the evening with a calming bedtime routine, such as taking a warm bath, and a cup of tea.

- Reading to promote self-care and self-love. I could have said watching a show or Netflix, but everyone knows how screen time at this hour messes up our melatonin (a hormone that regulates night and day cycles or sleep-wake cycles).

By implementing these basic and daily routines, you can prioritize your well-being and promote self-love as a daily practice until it becomes ingrained and you do not have to consciously do them. You will begin to notice that, with time, these little things have impacted you in a significant manner. Remember, this is just the foundation of the building because until and unless you are able to value yourself and put yourself before other people who do not mean anything to you, you will not be able to move ahead.

Once you have arrived at an optimal position of valuing yourself and have begun to grow positively, you can start to focus on your goals which may be short-term or long-term. For some people, the process can go simultaneously. They can work on strengthening themselves and establishing and achieving goals side by side. But if you feel you have difficulty focusing on more than one thing at a time, I would suggest you keep it simple and take one thing at a time, so you do not feel overwhelmed and end up being irate. Sometimes trying to do so much at one time bogs you down, and you end up becoming a jack of all trades and master of none. Remember, this is just the foundation of the building-up process because until and unless you are able to value yourself and create boundaries for others who intend to take your time and energy without reciprocation, you will not be able to move ahead.

It is noteworthy that setting and accomplishing short-term goals contribute to your overall motivation and impacts your long terms goals because, in truth, your short-term goals are milestones of your long-term goals. For example, if you intend to pursue a Ph.D. which is your long-term goal, your short terms goals would be attending junior high school, high school, and college and pursuing a master's degree until you reach Ph.D.

Similarly, if you want to set aside an amount of money to be used in times of emergency or maybe buy yourself a house, you may not have that kind of money at once. Buying a house can be your long-term goal, and you can break it into milestones and set short-term goals to be achieved on a daily, weekly, monthly, or yearly basis.

Perhaps you can set a short-term goal to save a portion of your income on a monthly or yearly to buy the house. Make sure that the goal set is realistic so that you have the motivation to pursue it. When you clear one step, you automatically get the motivation to move and accomplish the next one too.

Given below is a worksheet of a short-term goal leading to the long-term and how you can track it. You may make your own to see how far you have come. Paste it somewhere in the house or work desk where you get to see and mark it every day to keep the Spirit going.

Hi,

My name is Lisa, and I am trying hard to complete reading a book that I bought a few days back. It is a 300 pages paperback, and I have only been able to read 50 pages. I have a tough routine because I work and look after my family. Since this book is highly recommended for those who are trying to strike the right balance between their work, family, and self, I believe it is a must-read for me. Therefore, I have decided to break down my goal of completing this book into smaller milestones by reading ten pages a day. I have made this chart to keep track of my progress, so I stay motivated. I color the tab when I have completed the set page numbers to be read on a specific day.

Day 1: Monday 1 - 10	Day 2: Tuesday 11 - 20	Day 3: Wednesday 21 - 30	Day 4: Thursday 31 - 40
Day 5: Friday 41 - 50	Day 6: Saturday 51 - 60	Day 7: Sunday 61 - 70	Day 8: Monday 71 - 80
Day 9: Tuesday 81 - 90	Day 10: Wednesday 91 - 100	Day 11: Thursday 101 - 110	Day 12: Friday 111 - 120
Day 13: Saturday 121 - 130	Day 14: Sunday 131 - 140	Day 15: Monday 141 - 150	Day 16: Tuesday 151 - 160
Day 17: Wednesday 161 - 170	Day 18: Thursday 171 - 180	Day 19: Friday 181 - 190	Day 20: Saturday 191 - 200
Day 21: Sunday 201 - 210	Day 22: Monday 211 - 220	Day 23: Tuesday 221 - 230	Day 24: Wednesday 231 - 240
Day 25: Thursday 241 - 250	Day 26: Friday 251 - 260	Day 27: Saturday 261 - 270	Day 28: Sunday 271 - 280
Day 29: Monday 281 - 290	Day 30: Tuesday 291 - 300		

By keeping track of your actions and advancements, you will realize how self-aware you have become; it helps you to fill in the lacking, and the habit of evaluating your short-term goals (such as reading progress in a day for Lisa) will allow you to become self-aware in other aspects of your life too.

Psychologists Shelley Duval and Robert Wicklund defined self-awareness as the "ability to focus on yourself and how your actions, thoughts, or emotions do or don't align with your internal standards. If you're highly self-aware, you can objectively evaluate yourself, manage your emotions, align your behavior with your values, and understand how others perceive you correctly."

It is a crucial skill for personal growth and development because it enables you to identify areas for improvement and make positive changes. It also allows you to communicate effectively with others and build stronger relationships, as you are more in touch with your own emotions and better able to understand those of others. This will foster healthy communication because you will be able to communicate clearly to others about how you feel and what you want. It requires a willingness to acknowledge and accept your own flaws and imperfections, which can be challenging but ultimately leads to greater self-acceptance and a more fulfilling life. Developing self-awareness can be a lifelong journey, but it is a critical step toward personal growth and achieving one's goals.

Therefore, step into the journey of self-awareness and learn to master your mind and emotions to transform your life. Here's a step-by-step guide to developing self-awareness that will help you take charge of your life:

Step 1: Take time for reflection.

- Find a quiet place where you can sit and think. Reflect on your thoughts, feelings, and behaviors.

Step 2: Observe your thoughts and feelings.

- Watch your thoughts as they arise and observe how you feel in response to them. Be aware of the patterns and habits that emerge.

Step 3: Practice mindfulness.

- Learn to be present at the moment and pay attention to your thoughts and feelings without judgment.

Step 4: Keep a journal.

- Writing down your thoughts and feelings is a great way to process and understand them.

Step 5: Seek feedback.

- Ask for feedback from others to gain a different perspective on how you are perceived.

Step 6: Analyze your experiences.

- Take time to reflect on your past experiences, both positive and negative, and analyze what you can learn from them.

Step 7: Embrace your strengths and weaknesses.

- Recognize your strengths and celebrate them. Acknowledge your weaknesses and work to improve them.

Step 8: Be patient and persistent.

- Developing self-awareness is an ongoing process, and it takes time and effort to achieve. Be patient with yourself and stay persistent in your efforts.

Self-awareness can be categorized into two types: public and private. Public self-awareness involves the awareness of how others perceive you, allowing you to navigate social situations and act accordingly. For example, when you're at a job interview and know how you're coming across to the interviewer. You may adjust your behavior, language, or dress to conform to the social norms and expectations of the interview setting. You may also avoid saying or doing anything that may be perceived as inappropriate or offensive. This kind of public self-awareness is essential in maintaining positive relationships and navigating social situations effectively. However, an excessive focus on public self-awareness can lead to self-consciousness, causing individuals to prioritize others' perceptions over their own authenticity.

Have you ever found yourself in a situation where you're feeling a certain emotion, and you take a moment to pause and reflect on it? That's an example of private self-awareness. For instance, imagine you're having an argument with someone, and you start to feel angry. With private self-awareness, you would take a step back, recognize your anger, and try to understand why you're feeling that way. You might ask yourself questions like, "Is this emotion justified in this situation?" or "What triggered this response?" By doing this, you can gain insight into your own emotions and learn how to manage them healthily and productively. You can develop your private self-awareness skills and lead a more fulfilling and authentic life with a little practice.

For those who may not feel self-aware but strive to be, the good news is that self-awareness is a skill that can be developed with practice and patience. By taking steps to improve your public and private self-awareness, you can gain insight into your thoughts, feelings, and behaviors and learn to navigate them more effectively. It's not about being perfect or having all the answers but about being willing to look within yourself and grow. You can gradually cultivate a deeper understanding of yourself and your inner world through journaling, seeking feedback, mindfulness practices, and other techniques. Remember, developing self-awareness is a journey; with consistent effort and self-compassion, you can achieve your goal.

Chapter 6: Create and Maintain Financial Health

In a world that is so cutthroat when it comes to expenses and making both ends, visualize a scenario where you are free from the constant worry and anxiety related to financial matters. Your income is sufficient to pay your bills, meet your daily needs, enjoy your hobbies, and more. I do not mean to say to hoard things that are not even necessary for you, but at least savor things that you really need and dearly want, be it for yourself or any of your loved ones. Additionally, you aim to efficiently handle your finances to make sure that you can lead the lifestyle you desire. Let me tell you that financial stability can make all of these things achievable.

Now everyone wants to have this magic formula, and for you to achieve it, it is essential to understand what it means and why it matters so you can work in the most effective way to establish one. Financial stability is a state of balance in which the financial system is able to function smoothly and withstand unexpected shocks or disruptions. Many people assume that having a super-elite lifestyle is the true manifestation of being financially stable which is not true at all. You know that you are financially stable when your everyday finances are not disrupted in times of contingencies. This is the simplest interpretation of your financial stability. If you are one of those, Congratulations, and if you are not, don't you worry. We will walk through a few steps and strategies that can help you gain insight into how you can work towards making your home financially stable.

To promote financial stability, you can take a proactive approach by following some key principles. It is important to adopt wise policies and sound regulatory frameworks to help manage risks and prevent financial instability. This might include setting clear goals, developing contingency plans, and establishing effective communication with people who are responsible for contributing to and maintaining finances with you.

Additionally, if you want to maintain financial stability, it is important to manage risks effectively. This means figuring out what could go wrong financially and taking steps to prevent it from happening. For example, you might spread your money across different types of investments, set aside money for emergencies, and avoid taking on too much debt. By managing your risks carefully, you can help protect your finances and maintain your stability over the long term.

Finally, it is important to stay informed about financial conditions and market trends so that you can make informed decisions and take appropriate action if needed, lest the investment you have made or a source of passive income that you have set up bring about counter effects. This might involve keeping up to date with financial news, seeking out professional advice, and monitoring your own financial situation regularly.

Investing smartly is undoubtedly one of the most effective ways to create wealth. In fact, it serves as the foundation upon which many other financial strategies are built. Just like the trunk of a tree from which several branches grow, smart investments form the backbone of a strong financial house. By making wise choices and staying disciplined in your approach, you can unlock the full potential of your money and build long-term wealth that can provide for you and your family for years to come. There is no better time to start investing than now. If you have not but want to grow your net worth and secure a brighter financial future,

There are various affordable ventures that you can take up based on your interest and budget. You can start by partaking with a friend or any other reliable and trustworthy ally. While it may seem daunting at first, investing doesn't have to be complicated or expensive. With a little bit of knowledge and some smart choices, you can get going and build a foundation on which you can further build a venture of your own from the profit you receive to be the heroine of your own story.

Let me share my experience with you to give you a better understanding of what I aim to establish. There was a time when I, too, struggled with finances; things would have been otherwise if I wouldn't have made the decision to drive the helm of my money myself. Smart choices and lots of self-control, especially in the initial years, are extremely crucial. Indeed, I encountered considerable challenges when it came to achieving financial stability over a prolonged period. Upon graduating from college, I held an idealistic belief that I would easily secure a fantastic job that would not only enable me to pay off my student loans but also cover all my living expenses, afford me opportunities to travel, and provide me with a comfortable life while simultaneously building up my retirement savings.

Unfortunately, despite my best efforts, my initial endeavors to establish financial stability were not fruitful, and I found myself changing careers frequently, hoping to land a job that would satisfy my financial expectations.

Nevertheless, I persisted in my quest for a more secure future for myself and my family, which eventually led me to pursue a specialized degree in graduate school. By earning this degree, I acquired the expertise to assist others while also providing financial stability for my family. In retrospect, I am grateful for my struggles as they led me to where I am today, and I am now better equipped to create a sustainable financial future for myself and my loved ones.

Today, I am in a better position and financially stable because I persevered through my academic pursuits and employment, making significant sacrifices to adhere to my budget while in graduate school. In my efforts to secure housing for my children within my means, I applied for assistance from Habitat for Humanity. Additionally, I equipped myself with knowledge of financial matters such as taxes, debt management, and investment strategies by attending classes. This is something I would highly encourage you to do. If you think you lack the knowledge and need proper guidance in the domain, take classes or perhaps attend free courses that will enlighten you on how to work around these matters. Through these efforts, I successfully managed my finances by saving appropriately, spending wisely, earning more, paying off debt, and making prudent investments.

I am confident that my experience will resonate with many of you. When we are in college, we often hold a naive belief that our hard work and unbridled enthusiasm will enable us to accomplish anything. However, as we enter the real world, we may begin to question our abilities when we fail to achieve the desired financial success, wondering whether we are indeed exerting ourselves enough. Nevertheless, it is crucial to understand that hard work and smart work are two essential components that must be combined to achieve success. They are like two halves of a whole, each integral to the other. Hard work helps to keep us grounded and committed to our values and principles, while smart work enables us to soar and reach new heights.

It is essential to balance both hard work and smart work to maximize our potential and attain success. While hard work is necessary, we must also work smartly, taking calculated risks and being strategic in our efforts. Only then can we unlock our full potential and achieve the success we desire. Remember, hard work and smart work must go hand in hand to attain success in both personal and professional life. Smart work encompasses investing in the right means as you continue to work hard.

iBonds:

One great option for investing is iBonds, which are a

type of government bond that offers a low-risk, high-reward opportunity for investors. These bonds are easy to purchase and offer a guaranteed rate of return, making them a great choice for anyone looking to build wealth over time. Having made a personal investment in an ibond, I highly recommend this option for those seeking to earn additional income from their savings. With a minimum investment of just $25, it is an accessible option that can accumulate higher interest rates than traditional savings accounts. Furthermore, the investment must remain untouched for a minimum of one year, but to maximize earnings and avoid penalties, it is advisable to leave it for five years. This approach can prove beneficial for individuals looking to save for a down payment on a small business loan or a retirement investment. So, if you are looking to invest in a simple yet lucrative strategy, an ibond could be a smart choice.

You can buy ibonds directly from the US Department of the Treasury through the TreasuryDirect website. To open a TreasuryDirect account and purchase ibonds, you will need to provide personal information, including your Social Security number and bank account information. Once you have created an account, you can purchase ibonds in any amount from $25 to $10,000 per year using a debit or savings account. It is important to note that ibonds are not sold through traditional brokerage firms or banks, and therefore, TreasuryDirect is the only official channel for purchasing ibonds.

Roth IRA:

Another smart investment option is a Roth IRA, which is a type of retirement account that allows you to save money tax-free. By contributing to a Roth IRA on a regular basis, you can build a sizable nest egg for your retirement years without having to worry about paying taxes on your earnings.

I have family members who have opted for self-directed Roth IRAs, which I believe are an excellent choice for small business owners and real estate investors seeking an investment account with considerable gains. One of the significant advantages of a self-directed Roth IRA is the option to borrow from it tax-free. This aspect can be highly beneficial for individuals seeking to invest in their businesses or properties while maintaining flexibility over their investment funds. If you are looking for a robust investment option with tax-free benefits, a self-directed Roth IRA could be an ideal choice.

Passive Income Ideas:

Alongside the more traditional investment options, there are also many passive income ideas that can help you generate wealth over time. You will have to be very patient when you initiate a passive income stream because it may take time until it blooms fully. These ideas generally require lesser financial investment but more of your time and efforts, still less than a typical job or career, making them an attractive choice for anyone looking to earn additional money without sacrificing all of their free time. Obviously! An open oven bakes no bread, so you will have to give up on some of your free time initially.

One option is to start a side hustle, which involves offering a product or service that can be marketed and sold to others. These products can be generated through third-party sources if you do not have the budget to establish your own inventory at the very start of the venture. This hustle could range from starting an Etsy shop or selling crafts online to offering freelance services such as writing, graphic design, or consulting. Pick up anything that you are good at and comes to you naturally so that you do not have to get into the hustle of production a lot. With a little bit of creativity, consistency, and dedication, a side hustle can become a profitable source of passive income that can supplement your primary job or even replace it altogether.

Another idea is to rent out a spare room on Airbnb, which is an online platform that connects travelers with people who have extra space in their homes. By offering a comfortable and welcoming space to travelers, you can earn a steady stream of passive income that can help you pay off debts, save for a big purchase, or simply pad your savings account. Additionally, investing in dividend-paying stocks or real estate is another effective way to create passive income. By purchasing shares of a company that pays regular dividends, you can earn a portion of the company's profits without having to actively manage the investment. Real estate can also be a great source of passive income, as you can purchase a property and rent it out to tenants for a steady stream of rental income.

Multi-level marketing (MLM) companies are a popular option, particularly in the booming health and wellness industry. Joining an MLM offers an opportunity to become a part of a community of like-minded individuals and help others achieve their health and wellness goals. There are also eco-friendly MLMs that provide sustainable, healthy products for families. If you are open to the idea of MLMs, it's important to choose a company that aligns with your interests and passions so that the work is enjoyable.

Have you ever thought about creating a product? Well, if you have, then another way to generate passive income is to create a product and sell it online or in your community. This could include books, art, photography, greeting cards, clothing, pet products, or promoting other people's products as an affiliate marketer.

Starting a blog or vlog and promoting products that you use or like can also generate passive income. Creating passive income streams can be a fun and creative outlet, especially when you have extra time while raising kids alone or co-parenting. Purchasing tax liens is another way to generate passive income, but it requires specific knowledge and expertise. It's advisable to take a class or two on the process before diving in.

One of the keys to successful investing is also keeping track of your finances. This means especially taking steps to monitor your credit score because credit score determines your purchasing power. Building positive credit by responsibly managing debt is essential to improving and enhancing your credit score. I learned this valuable lesson from my past failures when I used credit cards to pay for my living expenses instead of investing in profitable opportunities. Next, you must create a budget and manage your debts and expenses effectively. By doing so, you can ensure that your investments are working for you and not against you and that you are on track to achieve your financial goals.

I can understand your struggle with how much of your hard-earned money to save versus invest. Don't worry; you are not alone! While there is no one-size-fits-all approach to financial planning, there are some general guidelines that can help you make informed decisions. To start, financial experts generally recommend saving at least 20% of your earnings. This may seem like a lot, but by putting aside a portion of your income each month into a savings account or other secure investment vehicle, you can build an emergency fund, cover unexpected expenses, or work towards specific financial goals like buying a house or taking a dream vacation.

You can save this amount in a money marketing account which is a type of deposit account offered by banks and other financial institutions. It is similar to a savings account but typically offers higher interest rates and some additional features. Money market accounts are designed for individuals or businesses that want to earn a competitive interest rate on their deposits while still having access to their funds in times of urgent need. They typically require a higher minimum balance than savings accounts and may have limited check-writing capabilities, generally up to six. But that should not be an issue because keeping the money moving is the key to moving forward to financial stability, and these accounts are nevertheless offering more flexibility in terms of access to funds than fixed deposit accounts.

Another good thing is that these money market accounts are FDIC-insured up to a certain amount, making them a relatively safe option. However, it is important to note that, unlike a savings account, money market accounts are not completely risk-free, and the interest rate can fluctuate depending on market conditions.

But what about investing? Well! The amount you should invest will depend on a variety of factors, including your age, risk tolerance, financial goals, and current financial situation. While there is no one-size-fits-all answer, many experts suggest investing at least 10-15% of your income in a diversified portfolio of stocks, bonds, and other securities.

Of course, the exact amount you save and invest will depend on your individual circumstances and goals. If you are just starting out and have a lot of debt to pay off, you may need to focus on saving before you start investing. Trust me, I have been in a situation of negative debt, and I would recommend that the first thing you do if you are in debt, is free yourself from this burden. However, I have come to understand that not all debt is created equal. There is a distinction between positive debt and negative debt. Positive debt is when you use a bank's money to purchase something that will yield a return, and you repay the borrowed funds over time. Negative debt, on the other hand, involves using borrowed funds to pay for something that does not generate a return.

It is essential to recognize the difference between these two types of debt. We should avoid using borrowed funds (negative debt) to pay our regular bills and expenses, as this can quickly spiral into a cycle of debt. However, borrowing to invest in a business, side hustle, or investment (positive debt) can be a wise financial decision if done correctly. When used strategically, positive debt can be a powerful tool to help grow our wealth and achieve financial goals.

On the other hand, if you are nearing retirement age, you may need to invest a higher percentage of your income to make up for the lost time. But do not let the numbers overwhelm you! By creating a budget, setting clear financial goals, and working with a financial advisor if needed, you can create a plan that works best for you because, ultimately, the key is to find a balance between saving and investing that works for you. Start today and take control of your financial future! By setting clear financial goals, creating a budget, and working with a financial advisor if needed, you can create a plan that helps you achieve your dreams while also ensuring financial stability and security for the future.

Lastly, teach your children the importance of responsible money management and the value of hard work. Consider establishing an incentive system in your household. This can be done on a weekly or monthly basis and can involve rewards for completing age-appropriate chores such as cleaning their room, doing laundry, or helping with dinner, which can help them understand the value of hard work and earn money to save or spend as they choose. Other means could be participating in extracurricular activities or achieving academic goals. By establishing a budget and rewards system, your children will gain a better understanding of how much money comes in and goes out for living and saving, and they will develop a sense of financial responsibility.

In addition to weekly allowances, consider offering incentives for extracurricular activities or family trips. For example, if your child participates in sports or music lessons, offer a reward for each practice or performance completed. This can be a small monetary reward or something like a favorite snack or dessert. When planning a family trip, set a budget for each child to spend on souvenirs or other treats during the trip.

This is because setting realistic objectives for your children to strive for and save for can also foster financial awareness and connection. By encouraging them to save for a specific goal, such as a new toy or a family vacation, they will learn the importance of delayed gratification and how to prioritize their spending. Additionally, establishing an incentive system and discussing financial goals with your children can be a starting point for meaningful conversations about money management and financial planning. By involving your children in these discussions and decisions, you can help them develop important financial skills that will serve them well throughout their lives.

Ultimately, the goal of budgeting rewards and incentives for your children is to teach them about financial responsibility while also encouraging positive behavior. By setting up a system of rewards and incentives, you can help your children learn the value of hard work, saving, and setting goals. Encouraging them to take an active role in managing their own money can also help them develop important financial skills that will serve them well in the future.

Chapter 7: Making a Career Work for You

Single moms face unique challenges as they have to shoulder the responsibilities of raising their children alone. One of the significant challenges that they face is financial stability. In the previous chapter, we talked about why achieving financial stability is crucial and how you can work your way toward becoming financially independent. I recall encouraging you all to initiate a venture of your own because it is a fulfilling and rewarding experience that leads to financial autonomy. However, it's not always feasible for everyone. There can be various constraints that might prevent someone from starting their own business, such as financial constraints, lack of experience, or limited resources. However, it's essential to work towards developing a successful career that can provide financial stability and help you achieve your goals.

A successful career can help you develop valuable skills, gain experience, and establish a professional network that can be beneficial in the long run. It will also provide financial security, which can help you support your family and achieve your personal and professional goals. Therefore, if you're not in a position to start your own business, focusing on developing a successful career can be a smart decision. It can help you build a solid foundation for your future endeavors and provide you with the resources you need to achieve your goals.

Here are some basic reasons why having a career is important for single moms:

- **Financial Independence:** A career can provide single moms with a stable source of income, which can help them support themselves and their children. It also provides them with financial independence, which can boost their confidence and self-esteem.

- **Role Modeling:** Having a career can serve as a positive example to their children, showing them the value of hard work, dedication, and self-sufficiency.

- **Career Advancement:** A career can offer opportunities for career advancement, allowing single moms to increase their earning potential and improve their financial situation.

- **Social Support:** A career can provide single moms with social support, a sense of purpose, and a feeling of belonging.

Welcome to the world of career self-discovery! It's an exciting journey where you get to explore your inner talents and passions to build a fulfilling and successful career. The secret to a healthy and long-term career lies in combining what you love with what you're good at - a concept that has been tried and tested by successful professionals and career experts alike. By aligning your natural abilities with your personal passions, you can unlock a world of satisfaction, fulfillment, and success in your work. And the best part? The process of identifying your strengths and interests is as exhilarating as it sounds! You get to explore various hobbies and interests to discover what truly resonates with your soul.

Of course, finding a career that works for you is not always easy. It may require some experimentation, networking, and ongoing learning and development. You might have to switch from career to career until you find the one that offers both personal and professional fulfillment. Ultimately, combining what one is good at with what you love will lead to a healthy and fulfilling long-term career.

It is a given fact that when you do the work that you a passionate about and skilled at, it's easier to stay motivated and engaged. You tend to be more innovative, productive, and effective in your work, which can lead to career advancement opportunities and increased financial rewards. As human beings, we all have a natural desire to grow and progress in our careers. We crave recognition for our hard work and the sense of accomplishment that comes from achieving our goals. Rewards and advancements in our professional careers can be powerful motivators, providing us with a sense of purpose and direction in our work.

When you receive recognition for your efforts, whether it be a promotion, a bonus, or simply a word of praise from your boss, it can boost your self-esteem and give you a sense of pride in your work. These positive emotions can lead to better mental health, and you feel more confident and capable in your abilities. You will have to discern which of these modes of recognition best aligns with your needs and values and shortlist a workplace that fulfills these needs. It may be that you are not really concerned with the advancement in position, but a raise in salary or an extra bonus would do for you. Or, perchance, you are okay with an average salary, but a word of praise is enough for you to keep going.

Still, at the end of the day, it is the money that you bring to the table that counts. At one point or the other, a word of recognition will no longer serve the purpose if your everyday needs aren't met because you all are toiling to fulfilling the responsibilities you have on your shoulder. Therefore, professional advancement will provide you with a greater sense of security and stability in your career than a word of recognition. Acclaim can serve to be your secondary need and priority but surely not first. As you progress up the ladder, you may have access to better benefits, higher salaries, more opportunities for growth and development, and leverage at work. This sense of security can help alleviate stress and anxiety, improving our overall mental health. Percase, then only appreciation would be more than enough for you.

While rewards and advancements can certainly be motivating, they should not be the sole focus of your career. It's essential to find a workplace that aligns with your values and passions and to cultivate positive relationships with your colleagues and superiors. By doing so, you can create a career that not only brings you success but also supports your mental and emotional well-being so you can continue with it in the long run.

I hope I have made it as plain as it could be that it's all about balance. The right balance between your desire for recognition and growth in your career with a healthy work-life balance is the key to a fulfilling and sustainable career. Take the time to explore your passions and values, and seek out opportunities that align with them. Building positive relationships with your colleagues and superiors and focusing on being a team player rather than just striving for personal success is yet another contributing factor in establishing a successful career because working in a career or workplace that feels unfulfilling or unsatisfying can lead to burnout, stress, and dissatisfaction.

In his book "Seven Habits of Highly Effective People," author Dr. Stephen R. Covey emphasizes the importance of beginning with the end in mind as the second habit of effective individuals. This is precisely what I am encouraging you to do: by envisioning what you want your career to look like and the outcomes you desire, you have a clear end goal in sight. The next step is to develop a strategic plan for achieving that goal. Determining what you need to achieve in order to get to your desired career position is an important step in creating a successful and fulfilling career. Here are some steps that can help you in this process:

1. **Step 1:**

   Identify your career interests and strengths: We have talked about it briefly how identifying your interests and strengths will help you understand what you enjoy doing and what you are good at. Therefore, take some time to reflect on your past experiences and identify the tasks and activities that you enjoyed and excelled at. This can be an activity you pursued while you were in high school or could be the idea of a venture that you always wanted to start.

Your education may seem to limit your career options, but it is important to keep in mind that sometimes it is perfectly okay to pursue a career that is different from what you studied in school. In fact, there are several reasons why this can be a wise decision, such as a change in interests and passions because it is common for individuals to develop new interests and passions over time. Since it may not align with your original field of study, pursuing a career that aligns with your current interests can lead to greater job satisfaction and a sense of fulfillment. Another reason could be transferable skills. Many skills learned in one field are transferable to other fields. For example, project management, communication, and leadership skills are valuable in almost any industry. Your education may have provided you with skills that can be applied to a wide range of careers. If one career league is not giving you enough opportunities for growth and learning, there is no harm in pursuing a career outside of your education for the sake of development. You may be exposed to new ideas and perspectives, learn new skills, and gain valuable experience that can be applied in the future.

While your education may have been a starting point, it does not have to dictate the rest of your career journey. It is okay to take a different career path if it aligns with your goals and aspirations and has a good market for it. Taking the Myers-Briggs personality career interest test can help you gain a better understanding of your personality traits and interests, which can, in turn, guide you toward career paths that align with your strengths and preferences.

2. **Step 2:**

   Research your desired career: Once you have identified your career interests and strengths, research the career that you want to pursue. O*Net Online might be your go-to platform to explore different careers and shortlist the ones that align with your interest and skills. O*NET (Occupational Information Network) is a comprehensive online database of occupational information developed by the US Department of Labor. It provides detailed information about hundreds of occupations, including job duties, required skills and knowledge, education and training requirements, and typical salaries. It allows you to explore different careers, identify related occupations, and make informed decisions about your education and career paths. Additionally, talk to people who work in the field, and attend industry events to gain a better understanding of the role. You might want to take up some ancillary courses to establish relevance to your career and make your profile strong enough.

3. **Step 3:**

   Create a career plan: Once you have researched your desired career, create a plan that outlines the steps you need to take to achieve your goal. This may involve gaining additional qualifications or experience, networking with industry professionals, or developing new skills. . LinkedIn has to be your best source for that. It is the ideal platform for career enhancement courses and networking. LinkedIn Learning provides a wide range of courses taught by industry experts that are tailored to your interests and career goals. In addition, LinkedIn allows you to connect with other professionals in your industry, join groups and communities, and participate in discussions and events, making it a valuable resource for networking.

4. **Step 4:**

Set realistic goals: When creating your career plan, it is important to set realistic goals that are achievable within a certain timeframe. Break down your long-term goal into smaller, achievable milestones and set deadlines for each one. If you do not seem to be achieving those milestones, it is time to sit and analyze whether the lacking is at your end or the company's end, and you might want to revise your goals or strategies depending on what is the need of the hour and what are the current circumstances. Sometimes you have to lose a battle to win the war, and sometimes, to get to some places, you have to leave some places.

A diary is your best friend in this situation; that will remind you about each and everything that you decided to achieve at the beginning of the journey. Don't we all feel the need to have a friend in such times who will be a non-judgmental sounding board and offer support and encouragement by reminding you about the motivation and determination you had at the start? A diary can be just that - a place where you can set your goals and brain dump and do your career planning., celebrate your successes, and learn from your failures. By regularly reviewing your planner and diary, you can stay on track with your goals and gain insights into your strengths and areas for improvement, ultimately helping you make progress in your career and life.

5. **Step 5:**

   Take action: To achieve success, taking action is crucial, and this requires discipline and a structured routine. Creating a routine that works with your responsibilities as a parent and effectively managing your time is key. By blocking out specific times to work on tasks and repeating this routine until completion, you can stay focused and make steady progress toward your goals.

   It's also important to prioritize self-care and relaxation, particularly on days off. Taking breaks and giving yourself time to recharge can actually increase your productivity and help you maintain your motivation over the long term. By balancing hard work and self-care, you can create a sustainable routine that supports your career and personal goals while also maintaining a healthy work-life balance.

   Remember, achieving your desired career position

requires hard work, dedication, and a willingness to learn and grow. Learning is a lifelong journey, and where you want your employer to advance you in your career, they might also want you to stay relevant to the work that you do and learn new skills that contribute to the growth and development of the company you are working for. The fact is that though apparently, you might be learning these new roles/skills for the sake of the career, in turn, you are the one benefitting from it. In case you have to move to another workplace or career line, this would be a plus for you.

Let's face the truth, if you want to stay ahead in your career and keep up with industry trends, learning new skills is a must. I understand that the thought of learning something new at work can be daunting for some of you. The good news is it's never too late to start learning, and there are many ways you can go about it.

First, take the initiative to seek out learning opportunities. Talk to your supervisor or HR department to see what training programs or resources are available to you. You can also search online for courses or tutorials related to the skill you want to learn. You will either have to pay for them or, depending on your financial condition, you may choose to take up those that are free of cost. If the ones that are really needed for your advancement, you may request your company to pay for them by briefing them on how this will benefit the company.

Next, break down the skill into smaller, more manageable tasks. This can make it less overwhelming and easier to tackle. Set achievable goals for yourself and track your progress to stay motivated. Remember to be patient with yourself. Learning something new takes time and effort. Don't be afraid to ask for help or guidance from colleagues or mentors who have experience in the skill you want to learn.

Finally, practice, practice, practice! Practice is key to mastering any new skill. Look for opportunities to apply the skill in your work or personal life. The more you practice, the more confident you will become. Don't let the fear of learning something new hold you back. Seek out opportunities, break down the skill into manageable tasks, be patient with yourself, and practice regularly. With these tips, you can successfully learn new skills and stay ahead in your career.

Above all, do not compare yourself with others, neither in terms of skills or salaries nor in terms of pace and progress. Remember, each one of you has your time to grow and bloom. Imagine two seeds of the same plant species planted in the same soil and exposed to the same amount of sunlight and water. Despite having the same conditions, one seed may grow faster and taller than the other, while the second seed may take longer to sprout and may grow at a slower rate. However, as time passes, the second seed may develop a stronger root system, enabling it to better withstand adverse weather conditions and grow more resiliently than the first seed.

In the long run, the second seed may even surpass the first seed in terms of size and strength, despite starting out slower. The first seed may have grown faster initially, but the second seed's slower growth allowed it to develop a more robust root system, making it more resilient and ultimately leading to greater long-term growth. It is not only about the timings, but circumstances and environment add a lot to your progress. Different kinds of seeds require different conditions to grow, which is why many of you will truly start to bloom when you either switch companies or career lines.

Therefore, dump the idea of comparing yourself with others and focus instead on taking inspiration from them, as it can be a powerful tool for personal growth and development. When you constantly compare yourselves to others, you become obsessed with measuring up to certain standards or achieving certain levels of success that are not even determined by you. This can often lead to feelings of inadequacy and self-doubt, and rather than focusing on what you have achieved so far and gaining motivation from it, you continue to get pissed and feel ungrateful. You will keep revolving around the same pattern.

Therefore, by shifting your focus from comparisons to inspiration, you can reframe your perspective and start to see the unique strengths and talents of others as sources of motivation and creativity. Rather than trying to compete with others or emulate their achievements, you can learn from their approaches and strategies and use them to enhance your own skills and abilities. For example, if you are an aspiring writer, rather than constantly comparing yourself to other writers and feeling discouraged by their accomplishments, you could start reading their work and studying their techniques to see how they approach storytelling and character development. By taking inspiration from their work, you can start to develop your own unique style and voice and use their success as motivation to keep pushing yourself to improve.

Ultimately, by focusing on inspiration rather than comparison, you can cultivate a mindset of growth and innovation and start to see the achievements of others not as threats or challenges but as opportunities to learn and grow. If there is someone you want to compare yourself to, let it be your old self. Compare yourself today's self with who you were a few days or weeks, perhaps months back, because it is your journey, and you need to see how much progress have you made in your path. "It's your journey-compete with yourself." Focus on your progress and growth rather than comparing yourself to others or seeking external validation. Set personal goals and benchmarks and strive to surpass your own achievements.

Make this your motto *"It's your journey; compete with yourself,"* and you will see yourself working towards becoming the better versions of yourselves and eventually the best version. This mindset invites you to take ownership of your lives, embrace your individuality, and focus on personal growth and improvement. Moreover, stay away from people who want to pull you down or belittle you. Let alone the idea of fighting them. Instead, be wise like a serpent and keep your distance from those who are a danger to your self-esteem and do not genuinely want to see you succeed. In contrast, surround yourself with a network of people who want to support you and help you in growing and teach you things that are helpful in your development. Network with people who are more than pleased to mentor you if needed and provide you with honest, professional advice and career guidance in case you feel you are becoming stagnant or feel that you aren't receiving your due share of growth and appraisals.

Moreover, this positive network will not only help you to improve your professional life, but through this positive network in your field of work, you will be able to help other amateurs and earn yourself good public relations in your field.

Chapter 8: Parenting with Love

Calling all adventure-loving parents! Buckle up because we are about to embark on a thrilling expedition into the magical realm of parenting with love. Think of it as an exhilarating roller coaster ride filled with heart-warming moments, unexpected twists, and a whole lot of laughter. As I navigate you through this wild terrain, you will discover the secret ingredients that make love the ultimate superpower in raising amazing kids. Get ready to don your cape, unleash your inner superhero, and let love guide you through the ups and downs of parenthood. So, grab your popcorn (and maybe a few tissues) because this chapter is going to take you on an unforgettable journey where love conquers all! Get ready for an adventure you won't want to miss!

Parenting is a journey filled with countless joys, challenges, and moments that shape the lives of both parents and children. Amidst the myriad of parenting philosophies and strategies, one timeless approach stands out: parenting with love. There is profound power in love to help you nurture and guide your children. Love forms the foundation of a strong parent-child bond, fostering trust, empathy, and emotional resilience. As you explore the depths of this essential ingredient, you will discover practical strategies, heartfelt anecdotes, and expert insights that will empower you to embrace the transformative force of love in your parenting journey. Get ready to take on a ride of knowledge that illuminates the path to creating a nurturing, compassionate, and harmonious family environment through the extraordinary power of love, which will walk you through the various facets of love. Prepare to immerse yourself in the wonderful world of parenthood, where you'll find a love unlike any other.

First things first, overviewing the concept of love. What is love? It is a magnificent and complex emotion that defies easy definition that has puzzled humanity for centuries. In its essence, love is a deep and profound emotional connection that transcends boundaries and unites people in a powerful way. It is a force that can bring immense joy, warmth, and fulfillment to our lives. Love encompasses a complex mix of emotions and actions that revolve around intimacy, passion, and commitment. It involves a deep sense of care, closeness, protection, attraction, affection, and trust. The intensity of love can vary and evolve over time, leading to a wide range of positive emotions like happiness, excitement, and fulfillment. However, it is important to acknowledge that love can also bring forth negative emotions such as jealousy and stress. Despite its significance and extensive research, love remains a deeply mysterious and elusive aspect of human experience, often defying complete understanding.

Love is a complex and multi-faceted emotion that takes on different forms in our lives. We experience love for various people, such as our partners and children. Although we use the same word, "love," to describe these feelings, the nature of the love we have for our partner and our child may differ. Nevertheless, we can confidently say that we love them both. In the realm of love, the Bible identifies four distinct types:

1. **Eros: (romantic or passionate love)** Song of Solomon (Song of Songs): This entire book in the Old Testament is a poetic depiction of romantic love between a bride and bridegroom.

2. **Storge: (familial love, natural affection)** Romans 12:10 and 1 Timothy 5:8.

3. **Philia: (brotherly or friendship love)** John 15:13 "Greater love has no one than this: to lay down one's life for one's friends."

Proverbs 18:24 ("One who has unreliable friends soon comes to ruin, but there is a friend who sticks closer than a brother."

4. **Agape: (unconditional, selfless love)** 1 Corinthians 13:4-: "Love is patient, love is kind. It does not envy, it does not boast, it is not proud. It does not dishonor others, it is not self-seeking, it is not easily angered, it keeps no record of wrongs. Love does not delight in evil but rejoices with the truth. It always protects, always trusts, always hopes, always perseveres." John 3:1: "For God so loved the world that he gave his one and only Son, that whoever believes in him shall not perish but have eternal life."

In this chapter, our focus is on exploring the concept of Storge, the love that arises within familial relationships. Storge, a term found in the Bible, may be unfamiliar to you. It refers to a specific kind of love—family love. The word, which has its roots in Greek, captures the natural and affectionate bond that forms between parents and children, as well as among siblings. It represents the deep and instinctual love that arises within familial relationships. While there is endless information present on love that can be discussed, I believe it is not necessary to go into the details of what you all are very well familiar with. Rather I would take time to talk about concepts that are misunderstood and not very commonly known.

Parenting is undeniably one of the most challenging journeys you can embark on, and the efforts and struggle double when you are a single parent, especially in the initial years. In the not-so-distant past, society had certain expectations for parents, often demanding a strict and emotionally distant approach. The prevailing belief was that raising children required discipline, control, and a firm hand. Parents were expected to maintain an authoritative stance, prioritizing rules and obedience over an emotional connection. However, times have changed, and with it, the understanding of effective parenting has evolved. Therefore you must recognize the importance of warmth, empathy, and emotional availability in raising healthy and well-adjusted children. The rigid and cold parenting style of yesteryears has given way to a more compassionate and nurturing approach, one that acknowledges the emotional needs of both children and parents alike. As you begin to practice this new approach, you will realize the transformative power of love, communication, and empathy, paving the way for healthy parenting that embraces the inherent challenges with compassion and understanding.

In the fascinating journey of parenting, you have

likely encountered the belief that too much of anything can be detrimental and unhealthy. In the past, there was a common misconception that excessive strictness could have adverse effects on your child's personality and mental health. In fact, even today, some even go as far as saying that if you scold or reprimand your children even for the wrongs they do, it means you did not truly love them. However, it is important to understand that love is not about giving in to every whim and desire of your kid, and allowing unlimited freedom and openness can actually have repercussions and may not be the healthy love that I encourage you to practice in your parenting approach.

Healthy love in a parenting approach is a beautiful balance of various elements that contribute to the well-being and growth of your child. It involves:

1. **Unconditional Acceptance:** Healthy love means accepting and embracing your child for who they are unconditionally. Often parents make the mistake of comparing one child with another; if you find yourself doing that, remember that is not healthy or real love that you have towards your child. You must recognize their individuality, strengths, and weaknesses without judgment or expectations.

2. **Emotional Connection:** Building a strong emotional bond with your child is crucial. Healthy love involves actively listening to their thoughts and feelings, empathizing with their experiences, and providing a safe space for them to express themselves openly. It means taking the time to truly listen to your children, validating their feelings, and guiding them with empathy and compassion. Let your child know that their feelings are valid and important. Avoid dismissing or downplaying their emotions. Instead, let them know you understand. Use phrases like, *"I can see that you are feeling sad/frustrated/excited about this,"* to show empathy and validate their emotional experiences.

If you downplay their emotions, your child will begin to be hesitant to share their emotions with you and might eventually stop coming to you. You need to understand that you have missed demonstrating healthy love, and even if you had a real love for them, you have failed at vividly communicating your love to them and giving them a sense of connection. It is crucial that your child is able to perceive your love towards them. Therefore, there will be times when you will have to love them in their love language.

3. **Nurturing Guidance:** Healthy love incorporates providing guidance and setting boundaries to help your child navigate the world around them. It involves offering support, encouragement, and gentle discipline that is focused on teaching rather than punishing.

Here is an example of how you can guide your child to promote love and discourage hitting their sibling when you discover that one of your children has hit the other:

    i. **Set the Context:** Set the context of love, respect, and kindness within the family by having a calm discussion.

    You: *"Our family is built on love, respect, and kindness. Let us find peaceful ways to resolve conflicts and treat each other kindly."*

    ii. **Teach Empathy:** Help your child understand the impact of their actions on their sibling's feelings by putting themselves in their sibling's shoes.

    You: *"Imagine how it feels to be on the receiving end of a hit. It can be really hurtful, both physically and emotionally. We* *want to create a safe and loving environment for everyone in the family."*

iii. **Express Expectations:** Clearly state that hitting is not acceptable and that there are alternative ways to express frustration or resolve conflicts.

You: *"Hitting is not an appropriate way to solve problems or express your feelings. Let us find healthier ways to communicate and work through conflicts together."*

iv. **Offer Problem-Solving Strategies:** Guide your child in finding alternative ways to express themselves or resolve conflicts peacefully. Teach them healthy coping strategies that will stick with them for a lifetime.

You: *"When you feel upset or angry, try using your words to express how you feel. We can practice taking deep breaths or taking a break to calm down before addressing the situation. You can also imagine as if you are being watched or recorded, and this will help you to use your* *words carefully and stay in the circle of respect. You all deserve respect, right?"*

v. **Encourage Love and Bonding:** Foster a sense of love and connection between your children by promoting activities that encourage cooperation, empathy, and positive interactions.

You: *"Let us find activities that can bring you closer together. How about reading a book together, playing a cooperative game, or working on a craft project where you can collaborate and enjoy each other's company?"*

vi. **Consistency and Reinforcement:** Be consistent in reinforcing these expectations and positive behaviors, offering praise and encouragement when your children interact lovingly and respectfully.

You: *"I am proud of you when I see you resolving conflicts peacefully and treating each other with kindness. Keep up the good work!"*

4. **Respectful Communication:** Healthy love encourages open and respectful communication between you and your child. It means actively listening to their perspectives, valuing their opinions, and engaging in constructive dialogue to foster mutual understanding, trust and promote confidence in your child. For instance, say your child, Sarah, expresses a different opinion on a family decision. Instead of dismissing or ignoring her perspective, you actively listen and engage in a constructive dialogue.

5. **Encouragement and Empowerment:** Real love involves empowering your child to explore their interests, pursue their passions, and develop their unique talents. It means providing guidance, support, and belief in their abilities to help them grow and thrive. For example, if your child's interest is in pottery, you can empower your child's pottery passion by creating a pottery space at home, providing necessary supplies, and enrolling them in pottery classes. Encourage their creativity, and connect them with pottery communities, where they can meet fellows from the same interest. Celebrate their work, and support their further learning. You

can even book a stall for them at a fair festival or carnival where they can sell the pieces of art they made.

6. **Setting an Example:** Healthy love requires modeling the behaviors and values you want your child to embody. Being a positive role model and demonstrating love, kindness, and respect in your own actions can have a profound impact on shaping your understanding of healthy relationships. Dealing with anger and hurt are two important things you would really want your child to learn right.

    One of the most effective ways to start is by recognizing and acknowledging your own emotions when you experience anger or hurt. This shows your child that it is normal to have these feelings. Next, demonstrate healthy coping mechanisms such as taking deep breaths, temporarily stepping away from the situation, or engaging in activities that help you calm down. By practicing these strategies in front of your child, you provide them with tangible examples of how to manage their own emotions. Additionally, engage in open and honest communication with your child about your feelings and how you navigate through them. This helps them understand that it is okay to express emotions and seek support when needed. Remember, your actions speak louder than words, so you empower your child to do the same by modeling healthy ways to handle anger and hurt.

Remember, healthy love in parenting is a dynamic and evolving process. It requires continuous learning and adaptation. By embracing these aspects of healthy love, you can create a nurturing and loving environment that fosters your child's emotional, social, and overall development.

Moreover, establishing a strong attachment with your child is crucial for a healthy and loving relationship. You will have difficulty communicating love or training your child if they do not feel connected to you. Attachment forms the foundation of emotional development, trust, and closeness. By consistently meeting their needs and responding to their cues, you create a sense of security and value. Since it is one of the key elements of the love process, attachment promotes emotional regulation, empathy, and healthy boundaries. It requires ongoing effort, adaptability, and understanding as your child grows. Prioritizing it strengthens your bond and sets the stage for a loving relationship that positively influences your and your child's life.

Edward John Mostyn Bowlby, a British

psychologist, psychiatrist, and psychoanalyst who is famous for his interest in child development, along with Mary Dinsmore Ainsworth, an American-Canadian developmental psychologist, proposed the Attachment theory. Healthy attachments and bonding, as understood in the context of Bowlby & Ainsworth attachment theory, refer to the development of secure and positive emotional connections between individuals, particularly between infants and their primary caregivers. He explained the innate need for human beings to form close relationships, primarily during infancy and early childhood, which significantly impact their social and emotional development.

According to Bowlby, healthy attachments are characterized by four key features. Since you would want your child to feel attached to you so that they can experience a sense of security and trust from you, you would want to learn about these four features to work around them.

- **Proximity Maintenance:** Infants and young children seek to stay physically close to their caregivers, as it provides them with a sense of safety and security. They engage in behaviors such as clinging, following, and crying to maintain proximity to their attachment figures. As a single mom, it can be challenging to balance the needs of your child with the demands of daily life. However, there are ways to work around the concept of proximity maintenance and still provide your child with a sense of safety and security, such as using baby carriers or slings, Practicing skin-to-skin contact, also known as kangaroo care, and establishing routines so set patterns.

- **Safe Haven:** Healthy attachments offer a safe haven for individuals when they feel threatened, scared, or anxious. The presence of a secure attachment figure provides comfort and reassurance, allowing the individual to explore the world with confidence.

  For example, your child clings to your leg, showing signs of distress, when you are leaving them at the daycare. Recognizing their anxiety, you crouch down to their level, offering comforting words and gentle touch instead of leaving them crying in the hands of the caregiver at the daycare.

- **Secure Base:** A secure attachment figure serves as a secure base from which individuals can explore their environment, knowing they have a reliable source of support to return to. This secure base encourages autonomy, curiosity, and independence in the individual. For example, your child may feel hesitant to proceed with a difficult task, but with your reassurance, your child gathers the confidence to continue and successfully tackles the obstacle. Your presence as a secure base allows them to explore and take risks, knowing that you are there to support and guide them in case they fumble.

- **Separation Distress:** When separated from their attachment figures, individuals may experience separation distress, which is a normal and expected reaction. This distress reflects the emotional bond and the desire to be reunited with the attachment figure, reinforcing the importance of the attachment relationship. For example, when you leave for work.

As a parent, it is crucial to understand how healthy attachments are built and how they can impact your child's emotional and social development. You can foster a secure attachment with your child by providing consistent and sensitive caregiving. Here is what you need to know:

1. **Secure Attachment:** Your goal is to help your child develop a secure attachment style. This means encouraging positive views of themselves and others. Be responsive to their needs, showing them that you're available and attentive. When they seek

support, provide comfort and reassurance, helping them build confidence in their relationships.

2. **Insecure Attachment:** This refers to patterns of attachment where individuals experience a sense of insecurity and uncertainty in their relationships even when they have grown up. Bowlby identified two main types of insecure attachment:

- **Anxious-Ambivalent/Resistant Attachment:** If your child shows signs of insecurity in relationships, such as excessive clinginess or fear of rejection, they may lean towards an anxious-ambivalent/resistant attachment style. Offer consistent support and reassurance, assuring them of your love and availability. Help them develop a sense of self-worth and build trust in their connections with others.

- **Avoidant Attachment:** If your child tends to withdraw from closeness or downplay the importance of relationships, they may lean towards an avoidant attachment style. Encourage healthy emotional expression and demonstrate the value of connection. Let them know that seeking comfort and support is normal and beneficial for their well-being.

- **Disorganized Attachment:** If your child displays contradictory behaviors or confusion in relationships, they may exhibit a disorganized attachment style. Be a source of stability and consistency for them. Provide a safe and nurturing environment where they can express their emotions and navigate their attachment needs with guidance and understanding.

You play a crucial role in shaping your child's attachment style. By being responsive, loving, and supportive, you can help them develop secure attachments that lay the foundation for healthy relationships throughout their lives.

While I have been talking about loving, developing healthy attachment, being responsive, supportive, respectful, and expressive, and reassuring your kids, many of you may have fallen into the trap of believing that I mean to say love is all roses and no thorns. When experts emphasize the fact that parents should always love their children and adapt to their needs for a healthy upbringing, many parents assume that we are talking about blindly following and agreeing to your kids' demands. Let me shed light on the truth that this is a misconception. When we say this, we mean that you should always have your children's best interests at heart and provide them with the love, care, and support they need to thrive. It implies that you have to be attuned to your child's needs and understand what is best for them.

For example, if your child wants to eat junk food all the time, you, as a loving parent, may need to say no and encourage healthier choices. Similarly, if your child wants to skip school, you, as a loving parent, would explain the importance of education and encourage them to attend. Your child will only be able to listen and agree to you if you have a strong bonding with them and if you have established a secure attachment with them. This takes us back to the first point, which is being supportive, loving, and expressive.

We must realize that love and discipline go hand in hand, and you must strive to strike the right balance. A healthy parent-child relationship involves setting boundaries and limits while also being supportive and nurturing so you raise up responsible and put-together individuals instead of insecure spoiled brats. For the same, it is crucial for you as a parent to know the difference between what love is and what love is not. Many parents fall into the trap of these myths and stereotypes, believing that they might fail as a parent if they do not make their kid's life a bed of roses. Since I do not want you to fall into this trap, I have discussed below some common misconceptions and myths about parental love so you can beware of them and keep away.

i. **Love means always saying "yes" to your child's requests or demands.**

While parents may want to fulfill their child's every request, it's important to set boundaries and provide guidance, even if it means saying "no" sometimes. Boundaries help children learn self-discipline and develop a sense of responsibility. For instance, if your child wants to stay up late and watch TV, you may be tempted to give in to their demands. However, as a parent, you know that getting enough sleep is important for your child's health and well-being. Instead of allowing them to stay up late, you can explain to your child why it's important to get enough sleep and establish a bedtime routine. You could suggest winding down activities like reading a book or taking a bath to help your child relax and prepare for bed. By setting this boundary and providing guidance, you are helping your child develop healthy habits and promoting their overall well-being.

ii.   **Love means never being angry with your child.**

Anger is a natural emotion, and it's normal for parents to get angry with their children from time to time. What's important is how parents express their anger and how they handle conflicts with their children. Here is an example: If your child repeatedly refuses to clean up their toys despite your repeated requests, you may feel angry or frustrated. However, instead of lashing out at your child or yelling, you can take a deep breath and calmly explain to them why it's important to clean up their toys. You could say something like, "*I understand that you're having fun playing with your toys, but it's important to put them away when you're done so that we don't trip over them and hurt ourselves.*" By expressing your anger in a calm and constructive way, you're teaching your child how to handle conflicts and resolve issues in a healthy manner. If your child is stubborn and does not understand your explanation, you can try using different methods of communication, offering choices such as *"Do you want to clean up your toys now or in 10 minutes, or do you want to put away the toys yourself or with me?"* Additionally, setting consequences for not following through with the request is another way to get them to listen to you, such as, *"You may lose the privilege of playing with the toys for a set amount of time or have to do an extra chore."* It's important for the consequences to be age-appropriate and for the child to understand the reason behind them. Remember to stay patient and consistent. If you fail to implement the consequences, your child may become even more stubborn, thinking that their mother/father will always let it be.

iii. **Love means always putting your child's needs before your own.**

Parents who neglect their own needs and well-being may become resentful and burn out. To avoid burnout and promote a balanced relationship, as a parent who is exhausted from work, you can prioritize self-care by finding a compromise that works for both you and your child. For example, if your child wants to play, you could suggest a quieter activity, such as a board game, rather than a more physically demanding activity or take a short break to recharge before engaging in playtime. By doing this, you model healthy behavior for your child and demonstrate the importance of self-care for effective caregiving. Taking care of yourself is an important part of being a good parent, and it can also serve as a positive role model for your child. This approach can help prevent burnout and promote a positive, balanced relationship between the parent and child.

iv.   **Love means never punishing your child.**

Discipline is an important part of parenting, and it can help children learn right from wrong and develop self-control. However, punishment should be used sparingly and in a way that is appropriate to the child's age and development. In the early years of development, generally, it is advised to discipline your child. Let's say a child has been acting out in class by disrupting their classmates and being disrespectful to the teacher. As a parent, you want to address this behavior and help the child understand why it is not acceptable. You could have a conversation with the child to understand why they are acting out and help them identify more appropriate ways to express themselves. You could also role-play different scenarios with the child to help them practice positive behavior and provide positive reinforcement when they show improvement.

On the other hand, if your teenager has been repeatedly breaking curfew and engaging in risky behavior, such as drinking and driving. As a parent, you have tried using discipline, such as having a conversation, setting consequences, and providing positive reinforcement, but the behavior has not improved and is putting the safety of the child and others at risk.

In this extreme case, punishment may be necessary, and you could include consequences such as temporarily revoking your teenager's driving privileges or seeking professional help, such as counseling or therapy. Remember that the goal of punishment, in this case, should be to address the behavior and help your teenager understand the severity of their actions rather than to simply retaliate or control them.

v. **Love is enough:**

While love is a critical component of a parent-child relationship, it is not always enough to ensure a healthy and happy relationship. Children also need guidance, discipline, and support to thrive. You must also provide your children with opportunities to learn, grow, and develop their own identities.

vi.   Showing love in different ways to children is favoritism:

It's important to remember that love is not a one-size-fits-all approach when it comes to parenting, and this means that as a parent, you must be able to adapt your approach to show love and affection in a way that best suits each child's unique personality, temperament, and needs.

As a parent, you must recognize that each child is different and may respond differently to physical touch, praise, and attention. Some children may require more independence and space, while others may need constant attention and support. It's your responsibility to understand and respect your child's individuality and adapt your parenting approach accordingly. You may be deceived into thinking that because you treat one child differently from another, you do not love them all equally and that you are prone to partiality. However, that is not the truth; as long as you are paying attention to every child's emotional and physical needs and helping all of them grow and thrive in a way that is best for them, you are doing just the right thing because every individual has a different love language and would

148

flourish only when communicated in that certain way.

As a parent, you are responsible for loving your child in the right way that is healthy and will lead them to be healthy adults with no pointless insecurities. In order to do so, you will have to pay close attention to the attachment style you foster in them during their formative years, which lays the foundation of how they connect with the people around them. Because anything and everything we do in this world involves people around us, it is crucial that your child is taught a healthy way to deal with the human aspects such as relationships, emotions, communication, behaviors, and love, lest they end up suffering when they reach in their adulthood.

Keep in mind that parents are role models and that you will have to demonstrate what you want your child to learn. Children imitate. Perhaps you will have to give up on a lot of your own habits to love your kid the right way and to rear them up in the best possible way. Parenting with love also means that you get into the process of learning every day to realize what works best for you and your child. However, in the race of all this, leaving your identity and your own being behind is not an ideal approach. Where it is important to strike a balance between love and discipline in your kids, it is also important to strike a balance between taking care of your kid/s and yourself. An empty jar cannot pour into a glass.

Chapter 9: Parenting with Autonomy and Healthy Discipline

Parenting with autonomy refers to a parenting style that prioritizes granting children a sense of independence, self-direction, and decision-making power within appropriate boundaries. It involves recognizing and respecting your child's individuality, unique needs, and capacity for making choices. Parenting with autonomy aims to nurture children's self-confidence, critical thinking skills, and ability to take responsibility for their actions.

In this parenting approach, you provide guidance and support while allowing your children the freedom to explore, make decisions, and learn from their experiences. Autonomy does not mean completely hands-off parenting, neglecting boundaries, or neglecting taking care of your children; rather, it involves finding a balance between offering guidance and granting your children the space to develop their judgment and decision-making abilities.

Imagine a dance floor where your child is the star performer. With autonomy as their partner, they learn to choreograph their own routines, expressing their individuality and finding their rhythm. As the supportive audience, you provide guidance and encouragement, celebrating their every step and applauding their courage to take center stage. In this symphony of parenting, your child becomes the maestro, directing their own journey of self-direction. You play the role of the conductor, providing the structure and harmony that allows their talents to flourish. Together, you create a harmonious melody of trust, respect, and open communication.

When you practice parenting with autonomy, it creates an environment that encourages open communication, mutual respect, and collaboration. You involve children in decision-making processes, provide age-appropriate choices, and value their children's perspectives. This approach recognizes that children have their own unique preferences, interests, and strengths and seeks to foster their independence and self-esteem.

Parenting with autonomy also emphasizes the importance of allowing your children to experience natural consequences and learn from their mistakes. Rather than shielding them from every difficulty or failure, you encourage your children to take responsibility for their actions and understand the outcomes of their choices.

Recognizing that mistakes are valuable stepping stones to learning and growth is crucial. Embracing the notion that children are permitted to make mistakes and subsequently learn from them is one of the fundamental principles. Through these experiences, your children develop resilience, problem-solving skills, and a profound understanding of the consequences of their actions.

Parenting with autonomy is a way of parenting. As a parent who adopts an autonomy-supportive approach, you prioritize your child's independence, individuality, and decision-making abilities. You provide guidance and support while allowing your child to explore and make choices based on their own interests and preferences. You offer explanations and opportunities for problem-solving and respect their opinions and perspectives. By fostering their autonomy, you believe in nurturing their self-direction and self-motivation, allowing them to learn from their experiences and develop their own unique identity.

Parents who empower their children help them develop a strong sense of self, make informed decisions, and navigate the world with confidence by fostering clarity in everything they do for their children and in everything they expect of their children. It supports their growth into independent, responsible individuals who can thrive and contribute to society because they know exactly what they must do and not do.

However, it is not always all roses and no thorns. There are also some styles and patterns in parenting that are unhealthy and do the opposite to your children. You must realize that the foundation of your child's personality, development, and well-being lies in the kind of parenting they receive; therefore, parenting styles play a crucial role in shaping a child's life. Understanding the different parenting styles can help you identify your own approach and make informed choices to foster a healthy parent-child relationship. Though it is a deep sea in itself that one can dive into, I have briefly discussed five common parenting styles to tell you the gist of it in a nutshell:

1. **Authoritarian parenting:** This style is characterized by strict rules, high expectations, and little room for flexibility. As an authoritarian parent, you may prioritize obedience and discipline, often using punishment to enforce rules. For example, you might set rigid curfews and expect unquestioned compliance from your child without offering explanations or considering their input.

   For example:

In the Anderson family, John is an authoritarian parent who tightly controls his daughter Emma's activities. He enforces a strict curfew, preventing her from spending time with friends or participating in extracurricular activities. When John discovered that Emma attended one of these activities against his rules, he had an explosive reaction and imposed severe repercussions on her. This authoritarian approach leaves Emma feeling restricted, unable to make her own choices, and fearful of expressing herself. The lack of autonomy and limited freedom within the household can hinder Emma's personal growth and independence.

2. **Permissive parenting:** With permissive parenting, the emphasis is on being nurturing and indulgent, allowing your child to have few boundaries or rules. You may avoid setting limits and instead prioritize your child's immediate desires and happiness.

For example:

Sarah as the parent who exhibits permissive parenting, often gives in to her child's demands for sweets or toys without considering the long-term impact on their behavior or well-being. Sarah quickly gives in to their demands to avoid a scene, buying them the desired toys whenever her child throws a tantrum in a store. This permissive approach can lead to the child developing a sense of entitlement and difficulty managing impulses. They may struggle with boundaries and have challenges understanding the consequences of their actions.

3. **Authoritative parenting:** Authoritative parenting strikes a balance between structure and nurturing. As an authoritative parent, you set clear expectations and boundaries while also being responsive to your child's needs and providing warmth and support. You establish rules and consequences but also encourage open communication and independence. For example, you might establish a consistent bedtime routine while allowing your child to have some choice in selecting bedtime stories.

   For example:

   An authoritative parent, Sarah maintains a healthy balance between structure and warmth in her parenting approach. When her child requests to go to a party on a school night, Sarah engages in a respectful conversation, considering the child's desire for socializing and the importance of academic responsibilities. They work together to establish a compromise that allows the child to attend the party while ensuring they complete their schoolwork beforehand. Sarah's open communication and willingness to listen foster a sense of autonomy and responsibility in her child.

4. **Uninvolved parenting:** This style is characterized by a lack of emotional involvement and neglect. Uninvolved parents may provide minimal supervision and support, leaving their children to fend for themselves. They may prioritize their own needs over their child's well-being. For instance, you might frequently be absent from your child's life, failing to provide necessary care, attention, or guidance.

For example:

Mark, an uninvolved parent, rarely engages with his child's life. He rarely attends school events or extracurricular activities and seldom provides emotional support or guidance. Mark is often preoccupied with his own interests and responsibilities, leaving his child feeling neglected and lacking in parental involvement. The child may struggle with a sense of abandonment and may seek attention and support from other sources outside the family.

5. **Helicopter parenting:** Helicopter parenting refers to an overly involved and overprotective style, where you hover over your child, constantly monitoring and controlling their activities. This can hinder their independence and self-confidence.

   For example:

   Meet Salena, a helicopter parent who is constantly hovering over her teenage son, Ethan. Sarah is excessively involved in every aspect of Ethan's life. She constantly monitors his activities, checking his homework, controlling his schedule, and even intervening in his social interactions. Salena is afraid to let Ethan make his own decisions or face challenges on his own. For instance, she insists on accompanying him to school events, micro-managing his friendships, and constantly stepping in to solve any problems he encounters. Salena's overprotective behavior limits Ethan's independence and hinders his ability to develop essential life skills and problem-solving abilities.

   It's important to recognize that there is no universal "correct" way to approach parenting, as what works for one family may not work for another. The key to effective parenting lies in being attuned to the unique needs of each child and fostering their emotional, social, and cognitive development accordingly. By adapting your parenting style to suit your children's individuality, you can create a nurturing and supportive environment that promotes their overall well-being. (Discover your dominant parenting style through a quiz at the end of the chapter).

Other than these parenting styles, there are other parenting patterns and behaviors found in the family dynamics that compromise the growth and development of your child, such as a parent-child relationship where the family dynamics are characterized by a lack of boundaries, resulting in a confusion of roles and expectations. This is known to be enmeshed parenting. Enmeshment can be simplified as an unhealthy state of codependence that restricts the independence of another individual. It is characterized by excessive involvement, intense control, and an overprotective nature, which greatly limits your child's autonomy and independence in decision-making. You can recognize if you are an enmeshed parent if you rely excessively on your children for support, hindering the emotional independence of your children and impeding their ability to form separate identities.

Here is an example of enmeshed parenting:

"A 25-year-old individual was hesitant about pursuing her dream career in the arts. Despite having a strong passion and talent for it, she found herself holding back. Upon exploring the underlying reasons, it became evident that her enmeshed relationship with her parent was a major contributing factor. The parent, who had always prioritized financial stability over personal fulfillment, constantly expressed concerns about the instability and uncertainty of a career in the arts. The individual, burdened by guilt and a fear of disappointing her parent, suppressed her own aspirations and settled for a more conventional career path.

This example showcases how enmeshed parenting can hinder personal growth and lead to individuals sacrificing their own dreams and needs to appease parental expectations. While many parents may think that this is what their children ought to do out of love for their parents, it is crucial to learn that enmeshment is not love, and one must not confuse it with love.

I understand that as a parent, it's natural for you to want the best for your child and show them love and care. However, it's important to recognize that true love goes beyond excessive involvement and control. Genuine love

160

respects boundaries and individuality and encourages healthy independence. Similarly, as a child, you may have grown up in an enmeshed environment where control and codependence were perceived as expressions of love. But now it is essential for you to unlearn that unhealthy pattern and beware and comprehend that codependence and enmeshment are not love; rather, they are dysfunctional mindsets of love.

Enmeshment and codependency share similarities as they both revolve around an unhealthy reliance on another person at an emotional or psychological level. Understanding the overlapping aspects of these concepts can shed light on the dynamics involved:

1. **Blurred boundaries:**

   Enmeshment and codependency entail a lack of clear boundaries between individuals, leading to a loss of personal identity and a fusion of needs. This can result in difficulties distinguishing one's own emotions and desires from those of the other person.

2. **Emotional fusion:**

   Both enmeshment and codependency involve a high degree of emotional entanglement, where one person's well-being becomes excessively dependent on the emotions and actions of the other person. This emotional fusion often leads to a sense of being enmeshed in each other's lives.

3. **Challenges with separation:**

Both enmeshment and codependency can create difficulties in establishing healthy separation and autonomy. Individuals may experience a fear of abandonment or feel incapable of functioning independently without the constant support or presence of the other person.

4. **Caretaking tendencies:**

Enmeshment and codependency often exhibit caretaking behaviors, where one person assumes a primary role in meeting the needs and desires of the other person. This can create an imbalanced dynamic where one party prioritizes the other's well-being over its own.

5. **Impact on mental health:**

Both enmeshment and codependency can have detrimental effects on mental health. Individuals involved in these patterns may experience heightened levels of anxiety, depression, low self-esteem, and difficulties forming healthy relationships outside the enmeshed or codependent dynamic.

It's worth emphasizing that while enmeshment and codependency share similarities, they are separate concepts that may necessitate varied approaches to healing and overcoming them. If you find yourself grappling with enmeshment or codependency, reaching out to a therapist or counselor can be beneficial. They can offer valuable support and guidance and assist you in cultivating healthy boundaries and fostering meaningful relationships. Remember, seeking professional help is an important step toward your well-being and personal growth.

Let us have a look at how enmeshment is different from codependency.

Differences	Enmeshment	Codependency
Focus of Dependency	In enmeshed parenting, the focus of dependency is primarily on the parent-child relationship. The parent becomes overly involved and enmeshed with the child, often neglecting	In codependent parenting, the focus of dependency extends beyond the parent-child relationship. Codependent parents tend to have dysfunctional relationships and may rely on others, such as a partner or family member, to fulfill their

	their own needs and boundaries.	emotional needs.
Boundaries and Independence	Enmeshed parenting is characterized by blurred boundaries, with little distinction between the parent and child. The child's individuality and independence may be compromised as the parent exerts excessive control and involvement in the child's life.	In codependent parenting, there may also be issues with boundaries, but the emphasis is more on the parent's own lack of personal boundaries and an overemphasis on caretaking and meeting the needs of others.
Relationship Patterns	Enmeshed parenting often leads to an intense, symbiotic relationship between parent and child, where	Codependent parenting, on the other hand, is characterized by a pattern of enabling and being overly reliant on others for emotional

	their identities become intertwined, and the child may struggle to develop a sense of autonomy.	validation and a sense of self-worth.
Impact on Children	Enmeshed parenting can result in children who have difficulty establishing healthy boundaries, expressing their own needs, and developing a strong sense of self. They may struggle with individuation and may have challenges in forming independent	Codependent parenting can also have negative effects on children, as they may internalize unhealthy relationship patterns and struggle with their own sense of self-worth and autonomy.

	relationships.	
Scope of Dependency.	Enmeshed parenting tends to be more focused on the parent-child relationship and may arise from a desire to protect or control the child.	Codependent parenting, on the other hand, extends beyond the parent-child relationship and may involve codependent patterns in other relationships as well.
Role Confusion	Enmeshed families may struggle with role confusion that typically arises from a lack of clear boundaries and individual autonomy. For example: In the enmeshed Smith family, unclear boundaries lead to muddled roles. John and Sarah depend on their	Codependency can lead to individuals neglecting their own roles and identities to accommodate the needs and expectations of others. For example, Laura, a codependent mother, prioritizes her son Alex's needs above her own. Seeking validation and approval from him, she neglects her own interests, hobbies, and personal growth. Her

	children for emotional support beyond their age, while Emily and Michael shoulder caregiving responsibilities. This neglects the children's development and hampers their autonomy and individual growth within the family dynamic.	identity revolves solely around being a mother, sacrificing her individuality and well-being in the process.

Additionally, in an enmeshed family, you may notice a tendency towards over-involvement, where family members become excessively entangled in each other's lives, leaving little space for personal privacy. Boundaries become hazy as your family intertwines their lives to an unhealthy extent. Moreover, individuals face challenges with expressing emotions, often leading to intense or inappropriate emotional reactions in various situations. You and your family members heavily rely on each other for emotional support, creating an imbalance and relying on others to navigate your individual emotional experiences.

It's essential to understand that love gives freedom and room to bloom, while enmeshment and codependency are unhealthy and destroy the emotional well-being of the child. When children are raised in an enmeshed environment with excessive control and codependency where their personal boundaries are not respected and their individuality is stifled, they lack personal identity contributing to their feelings of confusion, low self-esteem, and difficulty in forming and maintaining healthy relationships, as they grow older. They have a constant need for validation and approval from enmeshed parents, making them insecure and hesitant to initiate anything in their lives, be it an activity or a relationship. This dependency, when it persists into adulthood, even hinders their ability to establish romantic relationships, and they may need constant reassurances and suggestions from their parent about how to cultivate their relationship and deal with the issues they face.

In addition, because of their inability to function independently, they constantly fall into the pit of mental health disorders such as anxiety, depression, and/or a personality disorder. The constant pressure to meet the expectations and demands of enmeshed parents and the inability to not be able to function adequately without them can result in chronic stress, emotional turmoil, and a sense of being trapped in an unhealthy dynamic.

Now that you are aware that codependency and enmeshment can be obstacles to establishing a healthy relationship with your child, it is crucial to embark on a journey of learning and reflecting authentic love. As a single mom, it's crucial for you to be mindful of your own life and behavioral patterns to prevent passing on your insecurities and dysfunctional attitudes to your children. I understand that your upbringing and the environment you lived in have shaped certain patterns and ingrained unhealthy behaviors in your mind. In fact, certain life events, such as becoming a single mom, may have contributed to tendencies of excessive dependence, over-caretaking, or struggling with setting boundaries and control.

Breaking this cycle is essential. While you may have valid complaints and feel constrained in various situations, it's important to take a moment to relax and disrupt the pattern. As I mentioned in the previous chapter, parenting is a process that involves not only implementing new learnings but also unlearning old behaviors and relearning healthier attitudes. This will enable you to create a peaceful home environment and raise mentally, physically, and emotionally healthy individuals. (Assess if you are being an enmeshed parent or have been raised by enmeshed parents through a simple questionnaire at the end of the chapter).

Remember, breaking the cycle requires self-awareness, self-reflection, and a commitment to personal growth. By consciously challenging and transforming your own patterns, you can create a positive and nurturing environment for yourself and your children. To do so, there is no harm in getting a professional to assist you in this journey of unlearning enmeshment and codependency and relearning healthy love. The therapist will be able to provide you with a tailored approach to address these patterns effectively.

Discussed below are a few general steps on how you can get out of an enmeshment mindset. While these are general steps you can take to start overcoming these unhealthy patterns, it's important to remember that everyone's experiences are unique, and a personalized approach is essential to target the root cause and keep from relapsing.

1. **Acknowledge the issue:** The first step is recognizing that there is a problem and the need for change. Consider seeking professional guidance from a therapist or counselor who specializes in parenting.

2. **Establish clear boundaries:** Identify areas where you may be overly involved in your child's life and work on setting healthy boundaries. Give your child space to make their own decisions and respect their individuality.

3. **Listen actively:** Take the time to genuinely listen to your child, understanding their needs and perspectives without judgment. Avoid dismissing or invalidating their feelings or opinions.

4. **Consistency is key:** Set clear rules and expectations for behavior and follow through with consistent consequences. Avoid making exceptions or giving in to your child's demands.

5. **Offer support and guidance:** While encouraging independence, be available to provide guidance and support when needed. Help your child develop problem-solving skills while encouraging their autonomy.

6. **Emphasize positive reinforcement:** Use praise and positive reinforcement to acknowledge and encourage good behavior and achievements. This helps boost your child's self-esteem and confidence.

7. **Prioritize self-care:** Taking care of your own well-being is crucial for effective parenting. Ensure you

get enough rest, engage in regular exercise, and seek support from your social network.

Lastly, while you are juggling between finding the parenting style that works best for your child/ren and trying to avoid or unlearn enmeshment or codependence, you can start with befriending your child on a lighter note until you manage to put all the pieces in their places. This can be done by striking a balance between simply being a supportive friend to your child and providing healthy discipline. It entails establishing a strong connection with your child, being their confidant, and fostering open communication. At the same time, it requires setting clear boundaries, guiding them toward responsible behavior, and teaching them important life lessons. Striking this balance allows you to create a nurturing and respectful parent-child relationship where you can be both a trusted ally and a responsible authority figure. Here are a few tips on how to do this:

1. **Cultivate presence and attentiveness:** Make a conscious effort to actively engage with your child's life, demonstrating genuine interest and providing undivided attention when they seek support or guidance.

2. **Foster clear and effective communication**: Utilize open and respectful communication to establish

172

boundaries and expectations for behavior. Consistently reinforce these guidelines, ensuring your child understands them.

3. **Offer genuine praise and positive reinforcement:** Recognize and celebrate your child's efforts and achievements, offering specific and meaningful feedback when they exhibit positive behavior or make progress towards their goals.

4. **Embrace discipline as a valuable learning opportunity:** When your child misbehaves, approach it as a chance for growth and understanding. Engage in open dialogue, discussing what went wrong, why it was unacceptable, and collaboratively exploring alternative choices for the future.

5. **Strive for fair and constructive consequences:** Avoid resorting to harsh or punitive punishment that can harm the parent-child relationship. Instead, focus on implementing fair consequences that encourage accountability, learning, and personal growth.

6. **Lead by example:** Be a positive role model by embodying the behaviors and values you wish to instill in your child. Demonstrate respect,

responsibility, and kindness in your interactions with them and in your interactions with others.

In conclusion, as we wrap up this after gaining an awareness of these various concepts involved in parenting, it is essential to emphasize the importance of compassion and emotional freedom within our relationships with our children. Allowing our children to express their emotions, including anger and other negative feelings, without feeling the immediate need to fix or resolve them fosters their emotional growth and development. Shifting from a fear mindset to a growth mindset enables us to create a nurturing environment where our children can explore their emotions and learn valuable lessons from them. By cultivating compassion and granting our children the space to express themselves authentically, we can lay the foundation for healthy and resilient individuals who confidently embrace their emotions and navigate life's challenges.

Parenting Styles Quiz

Dear Readers,

This questionnaire is designed to help you determine your parenting style. Please carefully follow the instructions provided below to complete the questionnaire accurately.

1. First, read each statement thoroughly. Each statement describes various parenting behaviors and approaches.

2. Rate your agreement with each statement using a 5-point Likert scale. The options are as follows: (1) Strongly Disagree, (2) Disagree, (3) Neither Agree nor Disagree, (4) Agree, and (5) Strongly Agree. Choose the response that best reflects your agreement with each statement.

3. As you respond to the statements, it is essential, to be honest and unbiased. Base your answers on your typical behavior as a parent rather than on how you aspire to be or how others perceive you.

4. Make sure to answer all the questions. Leaving any statements unanswered may impact the accuracy of the results.

5. Consider each statement independently. Avoid letting your response to one statement influence your

response to another. Evaluate each statement based on its own merits.

6. Rate your answers based on your overall tendencies as a parent. Even if you exhibit behaviors associated with multiple parenting styles, select the response that aligns most closely with your predominant approach.

7. Lastly, when you have completed all the statements, review your results. You will receive a score for each parenting style based on your ratings. The parenting style with the highest score indicates your dominant approach.

Note: Please remember that this questionnaire serves an informational purpose only and should not be used as the sole determinant of your parenting style. For a comprehensive understanding of your parenting approach, we recommend seeking additional resources and professional guidance.

Thank you for your valuable participation in this questionnaire!

Question 1: I expect my child to follow strict rules without question

5 Strongly Agree	4 Agree	3 Neither Or N/A	2 Disagree	1 Strongly Disagree

Question 2: I tend to punish my child for their mistakes rather than explain the consequences.

5 Strongly Agree	4 Agree	3 Neither Or N/A	2 Disagree	1 Strongly Disagree

Question 3: I believe that children should always obey their parents without questioning their decisions.

5 Strongly Agree	4 Agree	3 Neither Or N/A	2 Disagree	1 Strongly Disagree

Question 4: I feel uncomfortable when my child challenges my authority or expresses their opinions.

5 Strongly Agree	4 Agree	3 Neither Or N/A	2 Disagree	1 Strongly Disagree

Question 5: I set high expectations for my child and demand excellence in all areas of their life.

5 Strongly Agree	4 Agree	3 Neither Or N/A	2 Disagree	1 Strongly Disagree

Question 6: I have difficulty setting boundaries or saying "no" to my child.

5 Strongly Agree	4 Agree	3 Neither Or N/A	2 Disagree	1 Strongly Disagree

Question 7: I am more likely to let my child do whatever they want without consequences.

5 Strongly Agree	4 Agree	3 Neither Or N/A	2 Disagree	1 Strongly Disagree

Question 8: I prioritize being my child's friend over being their parent.

5 Strongly Agree	4 Agree	3 Neither Or N/A	2 Disagree	1 Strongly Disagree

Question 9: I am hesitant to enforce rules because I want to avoid conflict with my child.

5	4	3	2	1
Strongly Agree	Agree	Neither Or N/A	Disagree	Strongly Disagree

Question 10: I often give in to my child's demands or requests, even if they are unreasonable.

5	4	3	2	1
Strongly Agree	Agree	Neither Or N/A	Disagree	Strongly Disagree

Question 11: I encourage open communication and discussion with my child.

5	4	3	2	1
Strongly Agree	Agree	Neither Or N/A	Disagree	Strongly Disagree

Question 12: I am responsive to my child's needs while still setting clear and reasonable expectations.

5	4	3	2	1
Strongly Agree	Agree	Neither Or N/A	Disagree	Strongly Disagree

Question 13: I provide consistent discipline and consequences for inappropriate behavior.

5 Strongly Agree	4 Agree	3 Neither Or N/A	2 Disagree	1 Strongly Disagree

Question 14: I give my child a sense of autonomy and encourage them to make decisions within limits.

5 Strongly Agree	4 Agree	3 Neither Or N/A	2 Disagree	1 Strongly Disagree

Question 15: I value my child's opinions and involve them in family decision-making processes.

5 Strongly Agree	4 Agree	3 Neither Or N/A	2 Disagree	1 Strongly Disagree

Question 16: I often neglect or pay little attention to my child's emotional needs.

5 Strongly Agree	4 Agree	3 Neither Or N/A	2 Disagree	1 Strongly Disagree

Question 17: I am frequently unaware of my child's activities, friends, or school performance.

5 Strongly Agree	4 Agree	3 Neither Or N/A	2 Disagree	1 Strongly Disagree

Question 18: I struggle to provide consistent discipline or fail to set clear expectations for my child.

5 Strongly Agree	4 Agree	3 Neither Or N/A	2 Disagree	1 Strongly Disagree

Question 19: I prioritize my own needs and interests over my child's well-being.

5 Strongly Agree	4 Agree	3 Neither Or N/A	2 Disagree	1 Strongly Disagree

Question 20: I am often physically or emotionally unavailable to my child.

5 Strongly Agree	4 Agree	3 Neither Or N/A	2 Disagree	1 Strongly Disagree

Question 21: I find it challenging to allow my child to handle tasks or problems independently.

5	4	3	2	1
Strongly Agree	Agree	Neither Or N/A	Disagree	Strongly Disagree

Question 22: I constantly monitor and oversee my child's activities and decisions.

5	4	3	2	1
Strongly Agree	Agree	Neither Or N/A	Disagree	Strongly Disagree

Question 23: I often intervene or solve problems for my child instead of letting them figure it out.

5	4	3	2	1
Strongly Agree	Agree	Neither Or N/A	Disagree	Strongly Disagree

Question 24: I have difficulty trusting my child's abilities to make their own choices.

5	4	3	2	1
Strongly Agree	Agree	Neither Or N/A	Disagree	Strongly Disagree

Question 25: I am overly involved in my child's academic performance and constantly seek updates from their teachers.

5	4	3	2	1
Strongly Agree	Agree	Neither Or N/A	Disagree	Strongly Disagree

Assessment Sheet for Enmeshment

Please read each statement carefully and choose either "Yes" or "No" based on your own experiences, thoughts, emotions, and feelings. It is important that your responses reflect your personal perspective. Be honest and take the time to self-reflect before answering each statement. In case you are unsure about a particular statement, please provide your best response based on your understanding. Your genuine input are greatly appreciated.

All the best and thank you for taking the time to complete this assessment.

S.No	Statement	Yes	No
1	Do you expect your child to follow the beliefs and values that you model?		
2	Do you encourage your child to pursue their dreams?		
3	Do you correlate self-worth to your child's achievements ?		
4	Do you encourage your child to have a healthy social life and develop relationships outside of the family?		
5	Do you consider your child as your friend and expect them to provide you with emotional support?		
6	Do you respect your child's personal boundaries and privacy?		
7	Do you allow your child to make their own decisions and choices within reasonable limits?		
8	Do you support and encourage your child's independence and self-reliance?		
9	Do you share personal information that should be kept private?		
10	Do you prioritize your child's emotional		

	well-being and encourage them to express their own emotions?		
11	Do you reward your child for behaviors that reinforce autonomy?		
12	Does your life revolve around the life of your child?		
13	Do you feel the need to know every detail about your child's life?		
14	Do you believe that you can provide all the support your child needs?		
15	Do you experience feelings of guilt when desiring personal space?		
16	Do you possess a strong understanding of your own identity?		
17	Do you perceive a sense of responsibility to help resolve all the challenges faced by your family members?		
18	Do you frequently evade conflict and encounter difficulty in asserting yourself by saying "no"?		
19	Do you put your child's needs before your own?		

Chapter 10: Dating and Co-Parenting

The intricate dance of dating while navigating the world of single parenthood is an adventurous balance to strike. As you decide to embark on this adventure, envision a life where love, connection, and harmonious co-parenting coexist in perfect harmony. How incredible would it be to create a fulfilling romantic relationship while fostering a healthy and supportive environment for your children?

In a society that might often portray dating and co-parenting as conflicting forces, it's time to challenge that narrative and discover a path that embraces both. Because let's be honest, no matter how tough a time romance may have given you in your past, the yearning for companionship and a romantic connection is inevitable. Picture this: you're a parent dedicated to providing a loving and stable environment for your children. At one point in life, you will feel both excited and apprehensive about venturing into the world of dating while also fulfilling your responsibilities as a co-parent. But fear not because you can create a beautiful blend of love, personal growth, and family harmony. Trust me, there is no harm in wanting to have a partner by your side, but this time, the dynamics are a bit different. You have another whole being attached to you who is impacted by the decision you make in your love life.

This chapter is your guide to finding balance, establishing boundaries, and building healthy relationships that nurture not only your romantic life but also the well-being of your children. It is important to dive deep into the intricacies of dating and co-parenting, offering guidance, insights, and practical tips to help you navigate this often-challenging terrain. We'll explore topics such as effective communication with your co-parent, introducing your children to a new partner, and setting healthy boundaries to ensure everyone's needs are met.

So, welcome to a new chapter of your personal growth journey with a concept that has the potential to transform your relationships and reshape your life: the idea of safe people/ person who is the ideal one to date. Keep in mind that you are not looking for perfection because no one is. You are aiming for the one who will fit well in your dynamics and with whom you can fit like a perfect interlock. Picture this: as a single mom navigating the challenges and joys of parenting on your own, how amazing would it be to have these safe people in your corner? Individual/s who genuinely care for you, support your dreams, and help you become the best version of yourself as you navigate the beautiful journey of motherhood.

In a world where connections are plentiful but true intimacy feels elusive, the importance of safe people cannot be overstated, especially for single moms like you. These are the ones who understand the unique struggles you face, the ones who create an environment where you can be vulnerable, where you can let your guard down and show your true colors without judgment. Safe people empower you to grow, heal, and thrive in ways you never thought were possible as you raise your children and build a fulfilling life for both yourself and your little ones.

But who are these safe people, and how do you find them? That's precisely what you'll explore on this journey. I'll guide you through the process of identifying these safe people, nurturing those relationships, and creating a family that uplifts and supports you every step of the way on your single mom journey. You would definitely not want to invite an unsafe person in your life who makes your life even tougher; hence it is essential to keenly analyze the fundamental dynamics and requirements before diving into this sea so you know clearly what you are looking for and what are the key indicators.

Safe People

Safe people play a pivotal role in shaping and influencing the person you were designed to be rather than simply accepting the person you are now. It is my sincere hope that you have become a safe haven for some individuals and that you are surrounded by safe people who uplift and support you on your journey.

Take a moment to explore the nourishing aspects that safe people bring into our lives.

1. They wholeheartedly accept us for who we are, embracing both our strengths and our flaws.

2. Safe people create an environment devoid of judgment, where we can freely express ourselves without fear of rejection or criticism.

3. They recognize that we are all a work in progress and extend their unconditional support, reminding us that it's okay to be imperfect and vulnerable.

4. Furthermore, safe people have the courage to provide us with honest feedback, even when it's difficult to hear.

5. They offer us the tough love and truth we need to grow and learn from our mistakes.

6. Their intentions are rooted in helping us become the best versions of ourselves, and they deliver their

guidance with kindness, empathy, and a genuine desire to see us thrive.

It's crucial to surround yourself with safe people who inspire and energize you. When you spend time with these individuals, you should feel uplifted, invigorated, and motivated to continue progressing on your personal growth journey. Their presence should leave a positive impact, reminding you that you have the power to influence one another towards becoming the individuals you were meant to be.

Unsafe People

Conversely, being around the wrong kinds of people can lead us astray and influence us to make poor decisions. Have you ever encountered individuals who drain your energy and leave you feeling exhausted or defeated? They are exactly the ones you need to stay away from. You will soon know the kind of energy they exert. However, your inclination toward them may take you longer to accept this is truly the case.

Being in the company of these individuals who bring you down can make you feel disconnected from your true self and hinder your progress. Your goal should always be to move forward, continuously evolve, and embrace your authentic self. Choosing the right people to surround yourself with is vital, but sometimes, you may struggle to make the best choices. Some of you have a tendency to attract such individuals who take advantage of your kindness and willingness to help, resulting in one-sided relationships where your needs are not reciprocated. This is a big red flag.

In the journey of building intimate relationships, it is crucial to acknowledge that everyone has their own weaknesses and areas for improvement. Perfection is an unattainable goal, and challenges are bound to arise along the way. That's why it's vital for you to seek a partner who is a safe person, dedicated to personal growth, and actively working on addressing their unhealthy attitudes and behaviors. How can you expect to effectively resolve your mutual issues with someone who is not even ready to acknowledge that their own actions or behaviors contribute to the problem? Under such circumstances, your attempt to bring peace and support to your life and your children can backfire. Therefore, instead of settling for someone who says, "This is how I am, take it or leave it," prioritize finding someone who genuinely wants to be in a relationship with you and is willing to put in the effort to better themselves. This mindset shift will empower you to seek a partnership that is built on mutual growth and the pursuit of a peaceful legacy together.

Peaceful legacy refers to the values, actions, and environment you would create for your children and the lasting impact it has on their lives. As single parents, you have a unique opportunity to cultivate a peaceful and nurturing atmosphere that promotes their well-being and prepares them to navigate the world with resilience and empathy. Building peaceful legacies involves utilizing morality as a guiding principle to prevent hatred and foster trust. By focusing on ethical values and healthy behavioral patterns, you can create positive and harmonious relationships that promote understanding, empathy, and cooperation.

When you enter the dating world as a single parent, cultivating a peaceful legacy can be challenging as your partner's involvement directly affects your child/ren. It's important to recognize that creating a harmonious environment now relies not only on your efforts but also on your partner's contributions. Together, you both play a significant role in building a peaceful legacy by fostering open communication, aligning your values, and actively working towards a nurturing and respectful atmosphere for your child/ren, which is why you want to date someone who is aligned with your values, shares the same vision and understands where you are coming from.

It is crucial to exercise caution and prioritize getting to well know a potential partner before introducing them to your children. It's essential to observe their past and present actions, As they can provide valuable insights into their character and compatibility as a long-term partner and potential step-parent.

Imagine their life as a garden: Are they planting the right seeds by making responsible choices and demonstrating integrity? Do they water and nurture their relationships by investing time and effort into building strong connections? Are they proactive in harvesting the fruits of their labor, showing that they follow through on their commitments and promises? Take note of their responsibilities and how they fulfill them. If they have children from a previous marriage, observe how they care for and prioritize their well-being. This can provide valuable insights into their parenting style and their ability to co-parent effectively.

Temperament is also a significant factor to consider. Look for signs of emotional stability and how they handle stress or conflicts. A partner who displays traits such as trust, respect, mindfulness, consideration, and a sense of duty towards themselves and others is more likely to contribute to a peaceful legacy.

Creating peaceful legacies involves being discerning and mindful of potential partners' character and actions. Trust is essential, and it is crucial to build it gradually by observing their consistency, integrity, and commitment to their words and actions. By taking the time to evaluate a potential partner's qualities, values, and behaviors, you can make informed decisions that prioritize the well-being and stability of your family. This approach can help prevent potential disasters, turmoil, and negative influences from entering your children's lives, fostering an environment of peace, harmony, and positive growth for everyone involved. As a single parent, you not only strive to shield your life and your children's life from unpleasant experiences but also desire a partner who shares the same vision to prevent disasters and turmoil.

There may be instances when you tend to like someone and see the potential goodness in them, which is at a mere distance from communicating your expectations to them. No wonder assertive communication can get you the deal. You all must be well aware of the importance of communication, so I am not getting into enlightenment. Rather what I want to guide you through is that assertive communication and cooperative behavior are essential elements for fostering a healthy and harmonious connection.

These practices promote mutual understanding, respect, and effective problem-solving, leading to a more fulfilling and sustainable partnership.

Assertive communication involves expressing your needs, desires, and boundaries in a clear and respectful manner while considering the feelings and perspectives of your partner. It allows you to assert your thoughts and feelings without aggression or passive passivity, creating an environment of open and honest dialogue. By practicing assertive communication, you can effectively communicate your expectations, resolve conflicts, and prevent misunderstandings from escalating. For example, as a single parent, an example of assertive communication could be discussing your need for dedicated quality time with your children and setting boundaries with your partner. You might say, "I value spending uninterrupted time with my children to strengthen our bond. It's important for me that we establish specific days or evenings where it's just us as a family. I hope you understand and respect this need for dedicated time with my kids."

In building a fulfilling and harmonious relationship as a single parent, embracing cooperative behavior is essential. By working together as a team and valuing the needs and desires of both you and your partner, you create a foundation of collaboration and understanding.

Cooperative behavior requires a genuine willingness to compromise and find solutions that benefit both parties. It means recognizing that your partner's perspective and desires are just as valid as your own. By actively listening and considering their needs, you foster an environment of mutual respect and support. Collaboration becomes key in navigating relationship challenges. Rather than approaching conflicts with a competitive mindset, you seek to find common ground and work towards mutually beneficial resolutions. This involves open and honest communication, where both you and your partner express your thoughts and feelings while actively seeking compromise.

By adopting a cooperative mindset, you nurture a sense of unity and shared responsibility within your relationship. Decision-making becomes a joint effort, with both partners having a voice and contributing to choices that affect your lives and the lives of your children. This promotes fairness, equality, and a deeper bond between you and your partner. Remember, embracing cooperative behavior takes effort and commitment from both partners. It requires active participation, empathy, and a willingness to find common ground. By cultivating a cooperative approach in your relationship, you lay the groundwork for a strong and supportive partnership that will positively impact your family's well-being and the peaceful legacy you aim to create.

Once you have carefully evaluated and assessed a potential suitor for a sufficient amount of time, you may find it helpful to refer to a checklist to determine if they possess the qualities necessary to be around your children (See this checklist at the end of the book). It's important to note that this checklist is not an absolute rule but rather a general guide based on commonly recognized principles that promote a healthy environment for children of single mothers. It's essential to remember that priorities and the level of significance placed on different qualities may vary from person to person. For some, effective communication may be fundamental, while for others, a strong sense of responsibility may matter the most. Ultimately, each individual should consider their unique circumstances and values when making decisions about introducing a potential partner to their children. If your potential suitor has managed to successfully check on the majority of the pointers in the list, it is time for you to introduce them to your child/ren.

Introducing Potential Suitor to Your Children.

There are 3 questions you need to ask yourself when you are planning to make the meeting arrangements. Who?

When? How?

The answer to who has already been discussed. Let's discuss When and How.

When & How:

When it comes to introducing a new partner to your children, it's essential to prioritize their emotional well-being. Take the time to let your children adjust to the reality of your single status. They need space to process the end of their relationship with their other parent and understand that there is no chance of reconciliation. Rushing into introducing a new partner can confuse and disrupt their already complex emotions. Avoid introducing your kids to potential short-term partners, as it can lead to more confusion and frustration. Instead, after the potential partner has passed the Who test and the initial honeymoon phase of the relationship has settled or at least become less intense is the time to introduce them to your children. You should have developed a serious and committed relationship by now.

Before the first meeting between your children and your new partner, it's important to approach the situation with care and consideration. Gradually introduce the idea of your new partner to your children by gently mentioning your "new friend" and highlighting common interests and enjoyable moments spent together. This gradual approach can help warm your children up to the idea of meeting your new partner, and they might even express curiosity or interest in meeting them.

If your co-parent is still involved in your children's lives, it's generally best to inform them about your new partner before the meeting takes place. Keeping your co-parent informed shows respect for their rights concerning the children and helps prevent potential conflicts or misunderstandings. Make sure to keep the conversation focused on how this information affects the children, keeping it matter-of-fact and respectful. By proactively sharing this news with your co-parent, you can avoid any negative feelings or accusations that could arise if they were to find out from the children or through other sources.

When it's time for the first meeting between your children and your new partner, it's important to keep things low-key and relaxed. Choose an activity for the meeting that allows everyone to feel comfortable and engaged, such as going bowling, watching a movie, or visiting a park. Avoid activities that may cause stress or restlessness, like long queues at amusement parks. By having an activity to focus on, you can help prevent awkward silences or uncomfortable moments that may occur when sitting around a dinner table with nothing else to do.

During the introduction, introduce your partner as a friend and keep the atmosphere casual. Avoid excessive displays of affection like kissing or holding each other. Instead, include everyone in the conversation and ensure everyone feels involved and heard. After some time, find a moment to step away briefly so your partner can interact with the children on their own. This allows them to establish a connection while also giving you some one-on-one time with your kids, just as you normally would.

Remember, the first meeting sets the tone for future interactions, so keeping things relaxed and inclusive is key. By creating an enjoyable and comfortable environment, you can help foster a positive connection between your new partner and your children.

Since there are some negative myths about step-parents, which may lead you to assume that your children will react poorly to your new partner, however, in reality, most kids simply want their parents to be happy. While they may be supportive of you meeting someone new, they may also struggle with how it will impact their relationship with you. If you have been single for a while, your children may have gotten used to having you all to themselves, and feelings of jealousy can arise. It's important to help them understand that a couple's relationship is different from the parent-child bond and reassure them that nothing will change between you and them.

As your relationship with your new partner develops, make sure to continue giving plenty of time and attention to your children. It's easy to become absorbed in a new relationship, but try not to neglect your kids in the process. They need to feel that they are always your top priority. This is especially crucial if you're soon to introduce them to someone who might seem like a threat to that sense of priority, even if it's just in their minds. Therefore it is essential to take the time to listen to your children's fears and concerns. Use reflective responding to show them that their thoughts and feelings are valid and that you hear them. Involve them in the problem-solving process by asking what they need and finding compromises together. Lastly, do not over-indulge your new partner in your family in the initial phase.

Trust me, it is a bad idea because it fosters your children's fears and aggravates their feelings of being neglected. You must ensure having one-on-one time with your children and have your partner join in on some occasions on a lighter level, introducing them as a friend. As time goes on, have a sit-down conversation with your children, using age-appropriate language, to explain your relationship. Their reaction is significant, and hopefully, by the time you have this conversation, they will have developed their own bond with your partner and accept them willingly.

If you and your partner decide to move in together, involve your children in the process. Give them a say in decorating the rooms that will be theirs in the new place, whether you're renting or buying. This will give them a sense of ownership in both the space and the relationship. If possible, discuss the move with your co-parent as a courtesy before they hear about it from the children. Open communication with your co-parent can help maintain a respectful and cooperative environment for everyone involved.

Remember, open and transparent communication with everyone, your children, their other parent, and your new partner is essential during this process. By being considerate and respectful in your approach, you can create a smoother transition and maintain a positive environment for all those involved.

SOME KEY ASPECTS OF A PEACEFUL LEGACY

Respect & Communication Respect and value each other's perspectives, needs, and boundaries. Establish mutual understanding, resolve conflicts, and maintain trust through open and honest communication. Actively listen and express yourself with kindness and empathy to build a foundation of respect and trust.

Empathy & Understanding: Practice empathy to connect with your partner or co-parent on a deeper level. Put yourself in their shoes, understand their emotions, and consider their experiences. Empathy fosters understanding, prevents misunderstandings and conflicts, and promotes forgiveness.

Shared Values & Morality: Build a peaceful legacy by aligning on shared values and moral principles. Prioritize honesty, integrity, fairness, and compassion. Let morality guide your decisions and choices, prioritizing the well-being of everyone involved.

Conflict Resolution: Approach conflicts with a problem-solving mindset instead of confrontation. Practice active listening, find common ground, and seek mutually beneficial solutions. Prevent hatred and nurture trust by resolving conflicts peacefully.

Co-Parenting with Cooperation: Nurture a peaceful legacy for your children through effective co-parenting. Cooperate, collaborate, and put your children's needs first. Maintain open communication, respect each other's roles as parents, and make joint decisions in the best interest of the child.

Continual Growth & Learning: Foster personal growth and self-reflection for a peaceful legacy. Acknowledge your mistakes, take responsibility for your actions, and actively work on self-improvement. Embrace a growth mindset to continually learn, adapt, and develop healthier and more fulfilling relationships.

Checklist: Determining Who Can Be Around Your Kids When Dating

Remember, this checklist serves as a guide to help you make informed decisions about who can be around your kids. It is important to trust your instincts and exercise caution when introducing potential suitors to your children. Prioritize open communication with your children and continually assess the compatibility and well-being of all involved parties as you navigate the dating process as a single mother.

☐ **Character Assessment:**

- Evaluate the person's character, values, and behavior to ensure they have a positive influence on your children.
- Consider factors such as honesty, integrity, empathy, and their ability to communicate effectively.

☐ **Trustworthiness:**

- Build trust with the person before introducing them to your children.
- Assess their reliability, consistency, and ability to keep commitments.

☐ **Child Safety:**

- Prioritize the safety and well-being of your children above all else.
- Ensure the person has a clean background check and no history of abusive behavior or criminal activity.

☐ **Emotional Stability:**

- Evaluate the person's emotional stability and their ability to handle stress and conflicts calmly.
- Look for signs of emotional maturity, resilience, and healthy coping mechanisms.

☐ **Compatibility with Your Parenting Style:**

- Consider whether the person's parenting style aligns with your own approach.
- Assess their willingness to respect your co-parenting arrangements and support your parenting decisions.

☐ **Respect for Boundaries:**

- Determine if the person respects and understands your boundaries as a parent.
- Assess their willingness to adhere to your rules and expectations regarding your children's well-being.

☐ **Compatibility with Your Values:**

- Ensure the person shares your core values and moral principles.
- Assess their views on important topics such as discipline, education, and overall family values.

☐ **Healthy Relationship Dynamics:**

- Observe how the person interacts with you and others.
- Look for signs of mutual respect, effective communication, and a willingness to work through challenges.

☐ **Positive Influence on Your Children:**

- Consider how the person's presence may positively impact your children's lives.
- Assess their ability to serve as a role model, mentor, or support system for your children.

☐ **Communication Skills:**

- Evaluate the person's communication skills, particularly when it comes to discussing sensitive topics with children.
- Assess their ability to listen actively, empathize, and communicate age-appropriate information.

Chapter 11: Manifest Your Destiny

Take a deep breath and close your eyes. Imagine a world where everything aligns perfectly, where you and your children thrive in every aspect of your lives. Picture it vividly – the location that resonates with your soul, the home that offers comfort and warmth, the relationships filled with love and support, the vibrant health that radiates from your very core, and the abundance that flows effortlessly into your finances. Manifest every single thing that you have been yearning for, learning, and working hard for.

Finally, the moment has come to release your desires into the universe. Take the time to visualize a future filled with happiness and health for you and your children. Be specific as you envision the ideal location, your dream home, nurturing relationships, vibrant health, and stable finances. This is your opportunity to harness the power of everything you have learned in the previous chapters, empowering you to manifest your destiny and shape a life beyond your wildest dreams. Welcome to the chapter of manifesting your desires, where you will utilize the wisdom gained from the entire book to unlock the incredible potential within you and create a reality that aligns with your deepest aspirations. With gratitude as your guide and self-compassion as your strength, initiate this venture of manifestation and fulfillment.

While many of you may wonder if it is too much to ask for or if the struggles of the present and past may hinder you from feeling the excitement that bubbles up within you as you want to realize that this vision can become your reality, let me encourage you with the fact that it all starts with your thoughts and beliefs. The book you are holding in your hand, which has come to an end, was once a mere thought until I decided to begin manifesting and working on it day and night. Remember that the universe is a vast and abundant place, and it eagerly awaits your command. There is so much that the universe has to offer – but to those who earnestly ask for it. Do not forget your mind is a powerful tool capable of shaping the world around you. It is time to harness that power and manifest your destiny.

Begin by embracing the concept of "as within, so without." Understand that your external reality is a reflection of your internal state. If you want to see positive changes in your life, you must first cultivate a positive mindset. Let go of any limiting beliefs that have held you back until now. Release the doubts, fears, and negative self-talk that have stood in your way. You are deserving of all the happiness, success, and abundance that life has to offer.

During their journey, the Israelites faced many trials and tribulations as they traveled through the desert toward the land of Canaan, the Promised Land. Despite experiencing miraculous events, witnessing divine interventions, and being guided by the wisdom of Moses, their progress was often hindered by their fearful and limiting minds. At times, the Israelites allowed their doubts and fears to overpower their faith and belief in the vision of a prosperous future. They questioned God's power and felt inadequate to overcome the challenges that lay ahead. These limiting beliefs and negative self-talk kept them from fully embracing their destiny as a chosen people, chosen to inherit a land flowing with milk and honey.

Recall when twelve spies were sent to explore the land of Canaan, ten returned with a report filled with fear and doubt, emphasizing the strong adversaries that inhabited the land. This negative perception spread among the people, and they became hesitant to proceed with their divine mission. Only Joshua and Caleb maintained a positive and unwavering mindset, recognizing the abundance and blessings that awaited them in the Promised Land. The consequence of their fearful and limiting minds was forty years of wandering in the desert, a journey that should have taken them a fraction of that time. It was only after a new generation, free from the mindset of their predecessors, emerged that the nation of Israel was able to conquer the Promised Land under Joshua's leadership.

This example of the nation of Israel serves as a powerful reminder of the significance of cultivating a positive mindset. When you allow fear and limiting beliefs to dominate your thoughts, you risk veering off course from your destined path. However, by fostering faith, courage, and a belief in your own abilities, you can overcome obstacles and embrace the abundance that life has in store for us. Just as the Israelites needed to shed their limiting beliefs to fulfill their divine purpose, we, too, must release any doubts that hold us back. Embrace the concept of "as within, so without," and understand that your internal state shapes your external reality. By nurturing a positive mindset and unwavering faith in your potential, you can conquer your own "Promised Land" and create a life of fulfillment and abundance.

However, sometimes it is the other way around. I remember I was once reading a blog online that stated how women often engage in self-care and physical transformation processes such as hair cuts or hair colors to overcome their inner negative and sad feelings such as a breakup. This transformation symbolizes a fresh start or a way of reclaiming their identity. In this way, they let go of the things of old and embrace a new look, even on the outside, so that they can feel more confident about the change they are trying to bring internally.

To your surprise, research does support the incredible power of self-care practices and personal grooming in enhancing your overall well-being and reducing stress levels. When you engage in self-care activities like exercise, relaxation techniques, spending quality time with loved ones, pursuing your favorite hobbies, skin care regimes, spa days, and hair treatments, you will find yourself better equipped to manage the emotions that arise during challenging times, such as heartbreak. Moreover, self-care is closely linked to boosting your self-esteem and empowering you with a sense of control over your life. Embrace the feeling of looking good and engaging in activities that promote self-confidence, as they can contribute to fostering a positive mindset and a more resilient approach to navigating those difficult emotions.

Now I must confess while there is limited direct research on the link between getting a new look and breakup stress, the broader body of research on self-care and stress reduction encourages you to prioritize taking care of yourself in various ways that suit you during times of emotional distress. So, remember, by making self-care a priority and embracing activities that bring you joy, you can effectively take one step closer to manifesting the life you want.

Therefore, recreating yourself with confidence and manifesting your ideal self and life is a transformative journey of personal growth and self-discovery, embracing change, both internally and externally, to become the best version of yourself. Here are some key areas to focus on as you embark on this empowering path:

1. **Personal Growth:** Start by setting personal development goals that align with your values and aspirations. Cultivate a growth mindset, embracing challenges as opportunities to learn and evolve. Engage in activities that nourish your mind, such as reading, attending workshops, or seeking guidance from mentors. Embrace new skills and knowledge that empower you to navigate life with confidence and resilience. Isolating is not really a good idea right after the precipitating event. Engage often with people who truly have your best interest at heart. Notice the message you would be giving out to the universe if you gave up on everything and cut off

from everyone. This does not mean that you must not spend time with yourself but make sure you are not mixing solitude with isolation.

2. **Hair:** A change in hairstyle or hair color can have a profound impact on your self-image. Experiment with different looks that resonate with your personality and enhance your confidence. Remember, it is not about conforming to societal standards but about expressing your authentic self through your hair choices. Hair is often seen as a reflection of one's identity and self-expression. Seeking a new look can be a way of reaffirming individuality and asserting independence. It serves as a physical manifestation of letting go of the past and moving forward with confidence. However, it is essential to remember that each person copes differently, and some mothers may choose other ways to prioritize their emotional well-being during this time of transition, and that is completely okay. Ultimately, the most important thing is to embrace self-compassion and find what brings you confidence and leads you to a winning and assertive mindset.

3. **Body:** Embrace body positivity and practice self-love. Focus on nourishing your body with healthy food and regular exercise, not with the aim of achieving a specific appearance but to feel strong and energetic. Dress in clothes that make you feel comfortable and confident, regardless of your body shape or size.

4. **Clothes:** Upgrade your wardrobe (if you can) with outfits that reflect your unique style and make you feel empowered. Dressing in clothes that align with your personality and aspirations can boost your confidence and leave a lasting impression on how you carry yourself.

5. **Language:** Pay attention to the way you speak about yourself and others. Use affirming and positive language that builds you and others up. Avoid self-criticism and negative self-talk, as they can erode your confidence. Practice speaking with clarity and assertiveness, expressing your thoughts and opinions confidently.

   For example Example: Instead of saying, "I am not good enough for this job," practice using affirming language and say, *"Though I may not have all the experience, I am eager to learn and grow in this role.*

I believe in my potential to succeed and will work hard to make a positive impact." When speaking about others, replace negative judgments with positive affirmations, such as, "She puts in the dedicated effort and has a natural flair for her work. I admire her determination and commitment to achieving her goals," instead of critiquing her weaknesses. By consciously choosing a positive and empowering language, you cultivate a more confident and optimistic outlook on yourself and those around you.

6. **Outlook:** Cultivate a positive outlook on life by focusing on gratitude and the abundance of opportunities around you. Challenge negative thought patterns and replace them with optimistic beliefs.

    For example, You may face a challenge pertaining to rearing a troublesome child. *"My child is always getting into trouble and never listens to me. I feel like I am failing as a parent."*

    You can replace it with an optimistic belief such as, *"Parenting can be challenging, but I am committed to learning and growing as a parent. I believe in my child's potential and know that with patience, understanding, and consistent guidance, you can overcome these challenges together."*

In this example, you may experience a negative thought pattern that leads to feelings of failure and frustration in your parenting role. However, by challenging this belief and embracing optimism in your child's potential and your ability to navigate challenges with patience and understanding, you can create a more positive and hopeful outlook on your parenting journey. This mindset will empower you to explore effective parenting strategies, seek support when needed, and nurture a strong and loving relationship with your child.

Lastly, surround yourself with positive influences and like-minded individuals who support your journey of self-recreation.

Remember, recreating yourself with confidence is not about conforming to external standards but about embracing your uniqueness and celebrating your individuality. Be patient with yourself and allow room for growth and evolution. The journey of manifesting self-recreation is a continuous process, and with each step you take, you will discover newfound confidence, strength, and authenticity that will radiate through every aspect of your life. Watch yourself and celebrate as you blossom into the person you have always envisioned.

Transforming your life and manifesting your desires will not happen overnight, and it is not always a piece of cake. Just like a seed that is sown in the ground, growth takes time. There will be ups and downs and moments when you might feel like the universe is not responding to your manifestations right away. You may find yourself facing challenges and feeling like you are falling apart. In such times it is crucial to provide yourself with constant reminders of your strength and resilience. One effective way to do this is by creating vision boards, a powerful tool to design and manifest your life.

A vision board is a visual representation of your goals, dreams, and affirmations. It serves as a daily reminder of the life you aspire to create. By pinning up positive affirmations, inspiring quotes, and images that represent your desires, you create a sacred space of motivation and encouragement. The process of creating a vision board is both therapeutic and empowering. As you curate the elements that resonate with your heart, you align yourself with the energy of your desires. This focused intention sends powerful signals to the universe, drawing your dreams closer to reality.

Whenever you feel overwhelmed or lose sight of your purpose, a quick glance at your vision board can recenter your focus and ignite your determination. It serves as a tangible source of inspiration, reminding you of your potential and the path you are forging. It allows you to dream boldly and fearlessly, trusting that you are worthy of the life you envision. The images and affirmations on the board reinforce the belief in your capabilities and remind you that you possess everything you need to overcome obstacles and achieve your goals.

To make the most of your vision board, place it in a space where you can see it daily. Allow yourself a few moments each day to absorb the energy it radiates and connect with the emotions tied to your desires. Visualize your dreams as if they have already come true, feeling the gratitude and joy of their manifestation. Have faith.

Consider the seed that has been planted. Initially, you will not see any visible changes on the surface. It takes time for the seed to absorb nutrients, develop roots, and slowly emerge from the ground. Similarly, your manifestations and goals might take time to materialize, but that does not mean they will not eventually blossom into reality. During this waiting period, it is essential to stay patient and persistent. Keep nurturing your desires with positive thoughts, actions, and unwavering belief in yourself. Just like a gardener tends to the seed, keep tending to your dreams and aspirations with love and care. Trust that the universe is working in mysterious ways, aligning the elements to bring your desires to fruition at the perfect time.

As you sow the seed of positive thoughts and an optimistic outlook in your life, it may seem like a small step at this moment. But just like a seed planted in fertile soil, when you entrust it to the hands of God and nurture it with faith and confidence, it has the potential to multiply beyond your imagination.

Remember the miracle of the 5 loaves and 2 fish when the apostles doubted that these meager provisions could feed the entire crowd? Similarly, you might feel uncertain that your positive thoughts and optimistic efforts will be enough to create the life you desire. However, when you have faith and surrender these resources to God's care, He can work miracles and multiply them beyond measure.

In your journey towards a blooming and happy life, keep in mind that the seeds of hope and trust you sow today will bear fruit in due time. Have confidence that God is aware of your desires and dreams, and He will provide the necessary nourishment and guidance to help them flourish. Stay patient and steadfast in your beliefs, even when it seems like progress is slow. Just as a seed takes time to grow into a strong and fruitful plant, your positive mindset and efforts will gradually yield results that align with your vision.

So, keep sowing those seeds of positivity and manifestations, knowing that in due time, they will sprout into a beautiful garden of blessings, nurtured by God's grace and multiplied beyond your expectations. Trust in the process, have faith and watch as your life unfolds into a magnificent tapestry of joy and abundance

Affordable Style Revamp

Thrifting and Secondhand Shopping: Explore thrift stores and secondhand shops in your area or online. You can often find stylish and unique pieces at a fraction of the cost of brand-new clothing. Thrifting allows you to experiment with different styles without breaking the bank.

Clothing Swaps: Organize a clothing swap with friends or family members. Everyone can bring clothes they no longer wear but are in good condition. This way, you can exchange items and revamp your wardrobe without spending money.

Basic Staples: Invest in a few versatile and timeless pieces that can be mixed and matched with various outfits. Classic items like a well-fitting pair of jeans, a white button-down shirt, or a little black dress can serve as the foundation of your wardrobe.

DIY and Repurposing: Get creative and repurpose your existing clothes. You can add patches, embroidery, or new buttons to transform an old item into something fresh and trendy.

Online Deals and Sales: Keep an eye out for online deals, discounts, and seasonal sales. Many retailers offer promotions, especially during clearance periods, which can help you snag stylish pieces at reduced prices.

Borrow or Rent: For special occasions or events, consider borrowing clothing from friends or family members. You can also explore clothing rental services, which allow you to wear designer pieces for a short period without committing to purchasing them.

Accessorize: Elevate your existing outfits with accessories like scarves, belts, jewelry, or hats. Accessories can add a unique touch to your look and help you express your personality without spending a lot.

Epilogue

As we reach the culmination of this remarkable journey, take a moment to reflect on the chapters that have shaped your path toward a life filled with purpose, growth, and joy. You embarked on this journey with the intention of crafting a life that aligns with your values and dreams, and the insights gained along the way have empowered you to do just that.

Throughout this book, you delved into the depths of personal and spiritual growth. From cultivating a spiritual connection to embracing self-care, positive relationships, and goal-setting, you have explored the vast landscape of personal growth. The subtle miracles, often unnoticed, reminded you of the constant divine presence in your life. These learnings have woven a tapestry of faith and gratitude that guides you each day.

The journey of reducing and managing stress became a pivotal chapter. Here, you broke the stigma of seeking help, recognizing that therapy and professional guidance are empowerment tools. By fostering rational thinking, regulating emotions, and practicing calming exercises, you have cultivated resilience in the face of life's challenges. Healing therapies and self-care practices have become your allies in nurturing your well-being.

In the stories of those who have walked this path before you, you have witnessed the tangible impact of these teachings. Individuals who have embraced the principles discussed here have experienced profound positive changes in their lives, from heightened well-being to stronger relationships and a greater sense of purpose.

In the realm of relationships, you learned to foster healthy connections. From parenting with love and autonomy to embracing the art of co-parenting and dating, you have nurtured the foundations of trust, open communication, and empathy. You have let go of toxic patterns, setting the stage for harmonious relationships based on mutual understanding and respect.

The exploration of intuitive goal-setting has allowed you to tap into your inner wisdom. By aligning with your passions and values, you have created a roadmap for personal growth and positive transformation. This journey has extended to your career as well, where you have harnessed your strengths, continued learning, and cultivated a supportive network. Financial health became a cornerstone, and you have embraced the principles of stability, wise investing, and budgeting. You have learned to create passive income streams and impart financial responsibility to your children, preparing them for a secure future.

Throughout this journey, the thread of positivity and optimism has been interwoven. You have aimed to rewrite your story as the hero of your life, or perhaps some of you already have during the reading phase as you touched upon finding joy in the simple pleasures, fostering gratitude, and manifesting your dreams through visualization and faith.

Hey dear Mommy, as you stand at the crossroads of your radiant life, remember that this journey is ongoing. Each chapter is not an end but a new beginning, an invitation to continue evolving, learning, and growing. The wisdom you have acquired will serve as a guiding light in moments of uncertainty and a wellspring of inspiration in times of need.

Start small with actionable steps that resonate with you. Practice daily prayer routines, engage in self-care rituals, and foster healthy relationships. Remember, each step you take brings you closer to the life you envision. You may at first choose a few specific steps from the book that resonates with you and commit to integrating them into your daily life. Whether it is starting a gratitude journal, engaging in regular meditation, or fostering open communication in your relationships, remember that each action propels you forward.

Remember, transformation takes time and is not without its challenges, and often good things do not come easy. There may be moments when doubt creeps in, or setbacks test your resolve. Embrace these moments as opportunities for growth. By staying committed to your journey, even in the face of adversity, you are sowing the seeds of lasting change. Hence, keep envisioning and manifesting the future you are grinding to craft. Let the love and compassion you have nurtured within yourself radiate outwards, touching the lives of those around you. Your story is one of empowerment, transformation, and the infinite potential that resides within every step you take.

May your days be filled with abundant blessings, and may you continue to navigate the beautiful tapestry of life with grace, resilience, and an unwavering belief in the magic of your own existence. Stay inspired, stay committed, and continue to embrace the infinite possibilities that await you.

With profound gratitude and boundless possibilities,
Heather Eden.

Page was intentionally left blank

APPENDIX

Assessing Your Parenting Style

To determine your dominant parenting style, follow these steps:

1. **Authoritarian Parenting**

Add up the number assigned to your responses for questions 1 to 5 because these 5 questions tap your tendencies for Authoritarian Parenting. For example,

1. If your response to question 1 was "*strongly agree,*" You will get 5 points because that is the point/number assigned to strongly agree in the questionnaire.

2. Similarly, if your response to question 2 was "*neutral,*" you will get 3 points.

3. The response for question 3 was "*disagree,*" you will score 2.

4. 4 for your response to question 4 if you ticked "*agree.*"

5. Lastly, if your response was "*strongly agree*" to question 5, you will get 5 points.

Now, adding these scores would be 5+3+2+4+5= 19 for Authoritarian Parenting.

Repeat the same for:

2.   Questions 6-10, they tap Permissive Parenting.
3.   Questions 11-15 tap Authoritative Parenting Style.
4.   Questions 16-20 are meant for Uninvolved Parenting.
5.   Questions 21-25 will give you a score for Helicopter Parenting.

By the end of the calculation, you should have 5 different scores, one for each parenting style. Just remember, the lowest score you can get for any parenting style is 5, and the highest is 25. After calculating the scores for each parenting style, consider the style with the highest score as your dominant parenting approach. Here's what each dominant style might suggest:

Authoritarian Dominance: A higher score in the Authoritarian section suggests that you might lean towards an Authoritarian parenting style. This could mean that you prioritize discipline and obedience but may have room to balance it with openness and communication.

Permissive Dominance: If your Permissive score is the highest, you might exhibit tendencies towards a Permissive parenting style. This indicates a tendency to allow your child considerable freedom but could also benefit from setting clearer boundaries.

Authoritative Dominance: A higher score in the Authoritative section indicates an Authoritative parenting

231

approach. This suggests a balanced style that encourages communication and autonomy while maintaining reasonable expectations.

Uninvolved Dominance: If your Uninvolved score is the highest, you may lean towards an Uninvolved parenting style. This style might benefit from greater emotional engagement and attention to your child's needs.

Helicopter Dominance: A higher score in the Helicopter section indicates a Helicopter parenting style. This suggests a strong involvement in your child's life but may benefit from allowing more autonomy and independence.

Correct Responses for Enmeshment Sheet

Listed below are the correct statements for enmeshment-related behaviors.

Yes, Statements for enmeshment-related behaviors

1. Do you expect your child to follow the beliefs and values that you model?
2. Do you encourage your child to pursue their dreams?
3. Do you correlate self-worth to your child's achievements ?
4. Does your life revolve around the life of your child?
5. Do you believe that you can provide all the support your child needs?
6. Do you feel the need to know every detail about your child's life?
7. Do you consider your child as your friend and expect them to provide you with emotional support?
8. Do you share personal information that should be kept private?
9. Do you experience feelings of guilt when desiring personal space?
10. Do you frequently evade conflict and encounter difficulty in asserting yourself by saying "no"?
11. Do you perceive a sense of responsibility to help resolve all the challenges faced by your family members?
12. Do you put your child's needs before your own?

No responses for healthy behaviors

13. Do you encourage your child to have a healthy social life and develop relationships outside of the family?
14. Do you respect your child's personal boundaries and privacy?
15. Do you allow your child to make their own decisions and choices within reasonable limits?
16. Do you support and encourage your child's independence and self-reliance?
17. Do you prioritize your child's emotional well-being and encourage them to express their own emotions?
18. Do you possess a strong understanding of your own identity?
19. Do you reward your child for behaviors that reinforce autonomy?

If a majority of your affirmative and negative answers align with the preceding responses, it could signal a heightened potential for enmeshment behaviors within your parent-child relationship.

Should your answers closely equate these responses in terms of quantity, it implies a well-proportioned dynamic in your parent-child relationship, which may signify commendable boundaries and emotional autonomy.

However, if fewer than half of your responses coincide with the provided answers, it suggests a more wholesome approach to your parent-child relationship, emphasizing both independence and robust boundaries.

Glossary

Adaptability: The ability to adjust to changing circumstances or situations.

Adrenaline: A hormone released in response to stress, increasing heart rate and alertness in preparation for physical action.

Affiliate Marketer: Someone who promotes products or services of other companies and earns a commission for each sale generated through their referral.

Agape: Unconditional and selfless love, often associated with a genuine concern for the well-being of others and a willingness to sacrifice for their benefit.

Airbnb: An online platform that allows people to list, discover, and book lodging accommodations around the world.

Anxiety: Feelings of unease, worry, or fear, often accompanied by physical symptoms like rapid heartbeat or restlessness.

Anxious-Ambivalent/Resistant Attachment: An insecure attachment style characterized by high anxiety and difficulty self-soothing.

Assertive Communication: A clear and respectful communication style that allows individuals to express their needs, feelings, and boundaries while respecting the rights and feelings of others.

Attachment: A deep emotional bond between individuals, often observed between parents and children.

Attention Span: The length of time one can focus on a task or topic without becoming distracted.

Authoritarian

Parenting: A parenting style marked by strict rules, discipline, and limited avenues for open communication between parents and children.

Authoritative Parenting: A well-balanced parenting approach that combines clear rules and expectations with warmth, open communication, and mutual respect.

Avoidant Attachment: An insecure attachment style marked by emotional distance and a reluctance to seek comfort from caregivers.

Behaviors: Observable actions, reactions, or conduct displayed by individuals in response to various situations, circumstances, or stimuli.

Biases: Preconceived notions or preferences that influence perceptions and decisions.

Bizarre: Extremely unusual or unconventional in a way that deviates from the norm or common expectations.

Borderline Personality Disorder: A mental health condition characterized by emotional instability, distorted self-image, and turbulent interpersonal relationships.

Burnout: A state of physical, mental, and emotional exhaustion caused by prolonged stress, excessive workload, and the feeling of being overwhelmed. It can result in reduced performance, decreased motivation, and a sense of detachment from one's responsibilities.

Catastrophizing: An irrational thought pattern where one magnifies potential negative outcomes.

Categorical Imperative: A moral principle that suggests one should act according to rules that could be universally applied, treating others as ends rather than means

Chronic Stress: Persistent and prolonged

stress can have negative effects on physical health, mental well-being, and overall quality of life.

Codependence: A relational pattern where individuals excessively depend on each other for emotional validation and support, potentially leading to unhealthy dependencies.

Codependent Parents: Parents who overly prioritize their children's needs to the detriment of their own well-being and boundaries.

Cognition: The mental processes of understanding, thinking, reasoning, and problem-solving.

Cognitive Distortions: Patterns of irrational thinking that contribute to negative emotions and behaviors.

Cognitive-Behavioral Techniques: Therapeutic strategies that focus on identifying and changing negative thought patterns and behaviors to promote emotional well-being.

Commercialism: A strong emphasis on business and profit-making, often at the expense of cultural or social values.

Compassionate: Showing kindness, empathy, and concern for others' well-being.

Contingency Plans: Pre-established strategies for handling unexpected events or emergencies that might impact your finances or life.

Co-Parenting: Sharing the responsibilities of parenting with a former partner, typically after a separation or divorce.

Coping Mechanisms: Adaptive strategies, behaviors, or actions that individuals use to effectively manage stress, challenges, and difficult emotions, aiming to maintain emotional well-being and resilience.

Cortisol: A hormone released in response to stress, playing a role in the body's stress response.

Counseling: A form of therapy where individuals receive guidance and support to address personal challenges and enhance their well-being.

Credit Score: A numerical representation of an individual's creditworthiness used by lenders to assess the risk of lending money.

Critical Thinking: The ability to analyze and evaluate information objectively and thoughtfully.

Cycle of Rumination: A repetitive pattern of overthinking and dwelling on negative thoughts or experiences, leading to heightened stress and emotional distress.

Data-Driven Decision-Making: Making choices based on factual information and data, ensuring informed and well-founded actions.

Deep Breathing: The practice of deliberately taking slow, controlled inhalations and exhalations to encourage relaxation, reduce stress, and promote a sense of calmness.

Depression: A mood disorder characterized by persistent feelings of sadness, hopelessness, and low energy.

Detoxification: The process of removing toxins or harmful substances from the body to promote overall health

Discipline: The practice of setting rules, boundaries, and consequences to guide behavior and promote self-control.

Disorganized Attachment: An insecure attachment style that combines anxious and avoidant behaviors, often linked to inconsistent caregiving.

Distorted Perceptions: Perceiving reality inaccurately due to biases, preconceived notions, or emotional influences.

Dividend-Paying Stocks: Stocks of companies that distribute a portion of their earnings to shareholders in the form of dividends.

Downplaying Emotions: Minimizing or dismissing the significance of one's feelings.

Emotional Availability: Being present and receptive to the emotions of oneself and others.

Emotional Disorders: Mental health conditions that primarily affect emotional regulation, such as anxiety or depression.

Emotional Entanglement: A state in which individuals' emotions become overly intertwined and interdependent, often resulting in difficulty distinguishing one's own emotions from others.

Emotional Turmoil: A state of inner emotional upheaval, often accompanied by heightened emotions, confusion, and inner conflict.

Emotional Well-being: The state of emotional health where one experiences a range of emotions in a healthy and balanced way.

Empathetic Living: A way of interacting with others that involves understanding their emotions and experiences and showing genuine empathy.

Empathy: The capacity to understand and share the feelings, emotions, and perspectives of others, fostering connection and compassion in relationships.

Enmeshment/Enmeshed Parenting: A relational dynamic where boundaries between parent and child become blurred, often leading to a lack of individual identity.

Equilibrium: A state of balance and stability, both emotionally and mentally, often associated with a sense of calm and well-being.

Eros: A form of love characterized by intense passion, desire, and physical attraction between individuals.

Etsy: An online marketplace where people can buy and sell unique handmade, vintage, or craft items.

Fight or Flight Response: The body's automatic response to perceived threats, preparing it to either confront the threat or flee from it.

Financial Autonomy: Having control and decision-making power over your own financial situation and choices.

Financial Independence: Achieving a state where you have enough resources to sustain your lifestyle without relying on external financial support.

Financial Stability: Having a secure and balanced financial situation where you can meet your needs and goals without excessive stress.

Frustration: Feelings of irritation or annoyance caused by obstacles, challenges, or unmet expectations.

Gratitude: A sense of thankfulness and appreciation for the positive aspects of life, both big and small.

Grounding Techniques: Approaches or exercises designed to help individuals reconnect with the present moment, fostering a sense of stability and reducing feelings of anxiety or dissociation.

Guided Imagery: A technique where a person is guided to imagine relaxing or positive scenarios.

Habitat for Humanity: A nonprofit organization that helps build and provide affordable housing for people in need.

Healing Therapies: Approaches or practices aimed at promoting physical, emotional, or mental healing.

Helicopter Parenting: A parenting pattern characterized by excessive hovering and overprotectiveness, potentially hindering children's autonomy.

Holistic Approach: Considering all aspects of an individual's well-being—physical, mental, emotional, and spiritual—when addressing health.

iBonds: A type of savings bond issued by the U.S. government that offers inflation protection and a fixed interest rate.

Impulsive: Acting without careful thought or consideration of consequences.

Insecure Attachment: A less confident emotional bond often resulting from inconsistent or unpredictable caregiving.

Intentional Breathing: Purposefully controlling one's breath to promote relaxation, stress reduction, and mindfulness.

Intrusive Thoughts: Unwanted and distressing thoughts that enter one's mind involuntarily and can cause anxiety or discomfort.

Intuition: Your inner sense or gut feeling about something without needing explicit reasoning, often based on your past experiences and knowledge.

Irrational Fears: Unreasonable and excessive fears or phobias that do not align with the actual threat level of the situation.

Irrational Thinking: Thought patterns that lack logical reasoning or factual basis, often leading to distorted perceptions and unnecessary anxiety.

Kangaroo Care: A method of holding and nurturing premature or newborn infants through skin-to-skin contact.

Like-Minded Individuals: People who share similar beliefs, values, interests, or goals, and who can offer mutual support and understanding.

LinkedIn: A professional networking platform where individuals can connect with others in their industry, showcase their skills, and explore job opportunities

Logical Analysis: A process of examining facts and information systematically to arrive at reasoned conclusions.

Love: An intense feeling of deep affection and care for someone or something.

Manifestation: The process of turning thoughts, desires, or intentions into reality by focusing on positive energy and belief in their realization.

Materialism: An excessive focus on material possessions and wealth, often overshadowing spiritual or emotional aspects of life.

Meditation: A practice of focusing your mind to achieve mental clarity, calmness, and self-awareness.

Mental Well-being: The state of mental health that involves feeling balanced, content, and able to cope with life's challenges.

Mindfulness: Being fully present and aware of your thoughts, emotions, and surroundings in the present moment.

Money Market Accounts Interest-bearing accounts that typically offer higher interest rates than traditional savings accounts.

Monkey Mind: A term used to describe a mind that is restless, jumping from thought to thought without focus or calm.

Mood: A temporary emotional state or feeling that can fluctuate throughout the day.

Motivation: The inner drive and enthusiasm that compel

individuals to pursue goals and take action to achieve desired outcomes.

Multi-Faceted: Having numerous different dimensions, aspects, or elements that contribute to a complex and comprehensive whole.

Multi-Level Marketing: A business model where salespeople earn income from their own sales and the sales of their recruited downline.

Negative Debt: Debt accrued from expenses that decrease your net worth, such as credit card debt or personal loans.

Negative Reinforcement: A behavioral principle where certain behavior is strengthened by removing or avoiding an unpleasant stimulus. This encourages the individual to repeat the behavior to prevent or escape the negative experience.

Nurturing: Providing care, support, and guidance to foster growth and development.

O*Net Online: An online resource that provides detailed information about various occupations, including required skills, tasks, and job outlook.

Optimism: A positive outlook on life that expects favorable outcomes and focuses on the potential for growth and improvement.

Overstimulated: Feeling overwhelmed or overburdened due to an excessive amount of sensory input, emotional stress, or stimuli.

Parasympathetic Nervous System: A division of the autonomic nervous system responsible for rest and relaxation responses.

Parenting with Autonomy: An approach to parenting that prioritizes fostering children's self-reliance and accountability while nurturing their individuality.

Parenting: The role and process of raising

and caring for children, encompassing nurturing, guidance, and support.

Passive Income: Earnings that you receive regularly with minimal effort after initially setting up an income source.

Peaceful Legacy: A positive and harmonious impact left on the world through one's actions, relationships, and values, contributing to a sense of peace and well-being for generations to come.

Permissive Parenting: A parenting style characterized by lenient rules and granting children high levels of freedom and autonomy.

Philia: Love based on camaraderie, loyalty, and mutual respect, often seen in strong friendships and partnerships.

Physical Well-being: The overall state of physical health, encompassing factors such as fitness, nutrition, and overall bodily functioning.

Positive Debt: Debt incurred for investments that have the potential to increase your net worth, such as student loans for education.

Positive Reinforcement: The practice of encouraging desired behaviors through rewards or positive consequences, reinforcing their repetition

Private Self-Awareness: Having insight into your own thoughts, feelings, and desires in a more personal and introspective way.

Proactively: Taking initiative and taking anticipatory actions to prevent issues or challenges, often involving forward-thinking and planning ahead.

Procrastination: The act of delaying or avoiding tasks or responsibilities, often leading to inefficiency and increased stress.

Progressive Muscle Relaxation: A relaxation technique

involving the gradual tensing and relaxing of muscle groups.

Promised Land: A metaphorical term often used to refer to a state of accomplishment, fulfillment, or success that one aims to achieve in one's personal journey.

Proximity Maintenance: Seeking physical closeness to a caregiver or attachment figure.

Public Self-Awareness: Understanding how you appear to others in social situations and how you're perceived.

Rational Thinking: A logical and balanced approach to evaluating situations and making decisions.

Reactive: Responding impulsively and emotionally to situations without thoughtful consideration.

Regulating Emotions: The ability to manage and control one's emotional responses in various situations.

Reinforcement: The process of encouraging or strengthening a behavior through rewards or consequences.

Relaxation: Techniques and practices used to release tension, reduce stress, and induce a state of calmness.

Resentment: Lingering feelings of anger, bitterness, or indignation toward a person or situation, often stemming from perceived mistreatment or unfairness.

Resilience: The ability to bounce back and adapt in the face of challenges, setbacks, or adversity.

Retirement: The phase of life when one stops working and lives on accumulated savings, pensions, or investments.

Ripple Effect: The idea that a single action can create a series of consequences or impacts that spread outward, much like ripples in water.

Roth IRA: A retirement savings account that allows individuals to contribute post-tax income and potentially enjoy tax-free withdrawals in retirement.

Safe People: Individuals who provide emotional support, respect boundaries, and promote healthy relationships, fostering a sense of security and trust.

Secularism: The idea of separating religious beliefs from government and public affairs, ensuring a neutral stance toward different beliefs.

Secure Attachment: A healthy and balanced emotional bond where a child feels safe and confident in their caregiver's presence.

Self-Acceptance: Embracing and valuing oneself, including one's strengths, weaknesses, and imperfections, without judgment or self-criticism.

Self-Care: Activities and practices undertaken to promote physical, mental, and emotional well-being and reduce stress.

Self-Control: The ability to manage and regulate one's own emotions, thoughts, and behaviors.

Self-Criticism: Judging oneself harshly and negatively, often leading to lowered self-esteem and increased stress.

Self-Direction: The innate capacity to independently navigate life's choices and make decisions aligned with personal values and aspirations.

Self-Discovery: The process of exploring and understanding one's own personality, values, strengths, and weaknesses.

Self-Doubt: A lack of confidence in one's abilities or decisions, often accompanied by negative self-perceptions and uncertainty.

Self-Esteem: A positive and realistic

perception of one's own worth and capabilities, contributing to a healthy self-image

Self-Love: Caring for and valuing yourself, embracing your strengths and weaknesses with compassion.

Self-Motivation: An internal propulsion that drives individuals to pursue goals with enthusiasm and dedication, stemming from inner desires rather than external pressures.

Self-Reflection: Thoughtful introspection and examination of one's thoughts, emotions, and actions.

Self-Respect: Treating yourself with esteem and honoring your values and boundaries.

Self-Worth: Recognizing your inherent value and understanding that you deserve respect and kindness.

Spoiled Brats: Informal term referring to children who are perceived as overly indulged and lacking in discipline.

Stereotypes: Widely held but oversimplified and generalized beliefs about a particular group or category of people.

Stigma: Negative attitudes or beliefs that create shame or discrimination around certain conditions or behaviors.

Storge: A type of love that is grounded in deep affection and familiarity, often found in familial relationships and close friendships.

Stress Management: Strategies and techniques used to reduce or cope with the impact of stress.

Stress: The body's response to challenges or demands, often resulting in emotional or physical tension.

Symbiotic Relationship: A close and interdependent relationship where individuals rely on each other for mutual support and benefit.

Sympathy:
Feeling compassion or pity for someone else's struggles or difficulties.

Taboo: A subject or action considered culturally or socially unacceptable or forbidden due to strong moral or societal standards.

Tax Liens: Government claims on the property due to unpaid taxes, which can result in the sale of the property to cover the tax debt.

Temperament: An individual's inherent and enduring emotional tendencies and behavioral patterns that influence how they react to situations and interact with others.

The Law of Attraction: The belief that positive or negative thoughts and emotions can attract corresponding experiences into one's life.

Therapeutic Techniques: Strategies and approaches used in therapy to help individuals improve their mental and emotional well-being.

Therapy: A structured process of seeking professional guidance and support to address psychological, emotional, or behavioral issues.

Traits: Distinctive and inherent qualities, characteristics, or attributes that contribute to defining an individual's personality and behavior.

Transferable Skills: Skills and abilities that can be applied and beneficial across different roles, industries, or situations.

TreasuryDirect: An online platform offered by the U.S. Department of the Treasury for buying and managing Treasury securities directly.

Triggers: Stimuli or situations that evoke strong emotional responses or memories.

Unconditional Acceptance: Accepting someone without conditions or judgment, regardless of their actions or choices.

Uninvolved Parenting: A parenting style where emotional involvement and guidance are minimal, often resulting in distant parent-child relationships.

Universal Law of Motion: A scientific principle stating that every action has an equal and opposite reaction governing how objects move.

Unsafe People: Individuals who exhibit toxic behavior, lack respect for boundaries, and contribute to unhealthy dynamics in relationships, leading to feelings of insecurity and mistrust.

Validation: Recognizing and acknowledging someone's feelings, experiences, or perspectives as valid and important.

Vision Board: A visual representation of goals, dreams, and desires, created by combining images, words, and affirmations on a board to serve as a constant reminder and source of motivation.

Visualization Techniques: Using mental imagery to create positive visualizations or scenarios.

Vulnerability: Being open and honest about one's feelings, thoughts, and experiences, even if they involve uncertainty or emotional risk.

Yoga: A physical and mental practice involving postures, breathing exercises, and meditation to promote relaxation, flexibility, and well-being.

www.ingramcontent.com/pod-product-compliance
Lightning Source LLC
Chambersburg PA
CBHW021616120626
46545CB00001B/261